Complete Poetical Works
and Selected Prose
of
George Bacovia, 1881-1957

Complete Poetical Works and Selected Prose of George Bacovia, 1881-1957

Translated by

Brenda Walker
and
Stelian Apostolescu

with an introduction by
Mihai Cimpoi

LONDON, CHESTER SPRINGS, BUCHAREST

2007

PUBLISHED BY
FOREST BOOKS

20 Douglas Road, Chingford, London E4 6DA UK
10 Ion Brezoianu Street
Sc. B, Apt 27-28
Bucharest
ROMANIA

Distributed by
Central Books
99 Wallis Road
London E9 5LN
UK
and
Dufour Editions
124 Byers Road PO Box 7
Chester Springs
Pennsylvania 19425-0007
USA

FIRST PUBLISHED
2007

Typset in Romania by Humanitas Multimedia, Bucharest
Printed in Great Britain by Polestar Wheatons Ltd, Exeter

Translation © Brenda Walker and Stelian Apostolescu
Photographs of Bacovia © Museum of Literature, Bucharest

ALL RIGHTS RESERVED

A CIP catalogue record for this book is available from the British Library

ISBN 978-1-85610-047-2

Cover drawing 'In vino Veritas' by George Bacovia

Contents

Autobiography, 1950 (Autobiografie)
by Gh. Vasiliu-Bacovia 7
Chronology.. 9
Translators' Notes 17
Introduction by Mihai Cimpoi...................... 21

Lead, 1916 (*Plumb*).................................. 37
Yellow Sparks, 1926 (*Scântei galbene*) 91
With You, 1930 (*Cu voi*) 135
In Fact Comedies, 1936 (*Comedii în fond*) 167
Bourgeois Verses, 1946 (*Stanțe burgheze*) 215
Verses and Poems, 1949–1957 (*Stanțe și versete*) 239
Other Verses, 1899–1957 (*Alte versete*)................ 303
Prose Poems. Night Pieces, 1926–1956 (*Bucăți de noapte*)... 341
Selected Short Prose (*Proză selectată*)................... 361
Final Considerations, 1954–1957 (*Considerații finale*)..... 381
Selection of Bacovia's drawings 396

Indices in English and Romanian 401

Self portrait

Autobiography

I was born in the year 1881, on the 4th day of September, to Dimitru Vasiliu, shopkeeper, and Zoia Vasiliu, housewife. Both are now buried in the town of Bacău. I was one of eight children of which only five survived. My two brothers and two sisters have all retired. I graduated from the Law Faculty and for most of the time was a clerk in the provinces and later, in the Capital. I married in 1928 and had only one son, Gabriel Vasiliu-Bacovia, now 19 years old. My wife, Agatha Vasiliu-Bacovia, born Grigorescu, a teacher and writer, is also retired.

Apart from my juridical knowledge, I have written literature for various reviews and publishers.

Gh. Vasiliu-Bacovia
[1950]

Chronology

1881
September 4th, a Friday, at 2.00 p.m., Gheorghie (as written on his birth certificate) was born to Dimitrie and Zoița Vasiliu in Bacău, Romania.

1888
He became ill and so he began school one year late.

1889
Sept 1st He entered the first class of School No 1 in Bacău.

1894
Aug 25th Gheorghe D. Vasiliu (note different spelling), entered the first class of the High School at the Gymnasium Principele Ferdinand, Bacău.

1899
He made his literary debut in *Literatorul,* Bucharest, with a poem *Și toate* ('And All') signed V. Gheorghe, Bacău, 1899.
May 9th He entered a competition for drawing held by the Society of Science and Literature Tinerimea română.
May 29th As a result of entering this competition, he received the first prize, with great accolade, floral crown and medal, at the Atheneum Concert Hall in Bucharest.

1899–1903
He repeated the 5th year of school, but completed the 6th year with average marks. He won a further prize for drawing but in the 7th year, he failed one of his final exams and had to retake this examination in the autumn.

1903
October 7th He entered the first year of the Faculty of Law at Bucharest University.

Dec 25th He published in the revue *Vieața Nouă* the poems *Amurg* ('Twilight'), *Lacustră* ('Lake Dwelling'), *Nevrosă* ('Neurosis'), and in the review *Arta*, the poems, *Toamnă* ('Autumn') and *Melancolie* ('Melancholy'). This was the first time he signed himself as G. Bacovia.

1904–1906
He continued to send poems for publication to *Arta*, *Mărgăritarul*, *Românul literar*, and *Liga conservatoare*.

1907
Now 26 years of age, he continued publishing the occasional poem.
February His poetry was noted for the first time by a critic in the review *Convorbiri critice*.
June 27th He was obliged to leave the Law Faculty of Bucharest due to bad marks.
December 1st He was admitted to the second year of the Faculty of Law but at the University of Iași.

1908
May 28th He entered for the 2nd year Law examinations but did not attend.
November 7th He asked to be entered into the 3rd year of study.

1909
September 21st He asked for entrance to the autumn sitting of the 2nd year examinations. His request was accepted, but he failed the exam.

1910
January 10th He asked for entrance to the Winter examinations' sitting. Again his request was accepted, but he was not successful.
May 28th He tried the second year examinations again at the summer sitting.
June 24th The examination commission decided to pass him with the lowest grade possible.

1911
January 11th He put himself on the list to be examined in the 3rd year that included graduation, for the Winter sitting.
February 9th He failed.
May 28th He asked to enter the summer sitting of the 3rd year examinations.
June 30th He failed.
September 20th He tried again for the autumn sitting.
November 5th The commission decided to pass him again with the lowest grade possible.
November 18th He received his Law Degree.

Chronology

1912
He continued to publish poems in literary magazines.
September 1st He started to work as an assistant teacher in various schools in Bacău.

1913
February 2nd He was appointed to the post of transcriber for the County Office in Bacău.
May 22nd He was appointed as assistant book-keeper at the same office.

1914
January 1st A productive year for him as a poet.
June He was admitted to the Hospital for Nervous Diseases in Bucharest.
December He returned to Bacău.

1915
May With some friends he started a the review *Orizonturi noi* with a modernist trend, in which many of his poems appeared.
An article appeared in the magazine *Cronica Moldovei* which spoke of Bacovia's miserable state of poverty.
September–December He published more poems in magazines.

1916
January His first volume of poetry *Plumb* ('Lead') appeared, published by Tipografia Flacăra. Many appreciative reviews followed.
June 23rd He was appointed to the post of transcriber in the Department of Education at the Ministry of Culture, Bucharest.

1920
He changed jobs and became Manager in the office of the Ministry of Works and Social Assistance.

1921
He was promoted in the same Ministry and published more poems in magazines.

1922
December 5th At a colloquium of literature held at Bucharest University's Faculty of Letters, a report was read on his volume *Plumb*.
He left Bucharest to live in Bacău.

1923
December 5th He visited Bucharest again where Agatha Grigorescu promised to marry him when she had completed her university studies. She visited him in Bacău in the following year.

1924
The second edition of *Plumb* is published.

1925
He became a teacher of drawing and calligraphy at the Normal School for Boys (a vocational school) in Bacău.
He received the Poetry Prize of the Society of Romanian Writers. Changed his job to be a teacher of drawing and calligraphy at the Commercial School in Bacău.

1926
Published the volume *Scântei galbene* ('Yellow Sparks') in *Tipografia Minerva*, Bacău.
Changed his job to teach at a different vocational school.

1927
He requested a job at the Ministry of Arts and Culture, Bucharest, using his success as a poet as a basis for his application.

1928
June 28th He married Agatha Grigorescu, fourteen years his junior. (She was born 1895 and died in 1981). They lived in Bucharest.
October 28th Agatha wrote to a member of the Romanian Academy, Liviu Rebreanu, saying that Bacovia was seriously ill, shouting, singing, and disturbing everybody. He was then admitted to a Psychiatric Clinic in Bucharest.
The volume, *Scântei galbene* was well received by the critics.

1929
He was now accepted as a good poet throughout the country and some of his poems were read on the radio.

1930
He published his third volume, *Cu voi* ('With You'), with the Orizonturi noi Publishing House. It too was well received.
Liviu Rebreanu informed King Carol I that George Bacovia was among 24 recipients of literary bursaries offered as support to writers in need.

1931
Summer The young family moved back to live in Bacău in what is today the Memorial House of George Bacovia.
November 8th Their only child Gabriel was born. (He died in Bacău, January 24th 1999 in great poverty).

Chronology 13

1932
March 24th King Carol awarded him, The Order of Merit (Second Class) for Letters and Literary Works.
December 19th The Society of Romanian Writers awarded him a pension to start from January 1933.

1933
February For three days he took part in a colloquium held in Bucharest where they discussed his poetical works.
July 2nd The building began on his house in Bucharest with money lent to Agatha by the Teachers' Trade Union This is now the Memorial House of Bacovia in Bucharest.
September The family moved to settle in Bucharest where Agatha became a teacher, and Bacovia was admitted to a Psychiatric Clinic.

1934
He shared the National Prize for Poetry with Tudor Arghezi.
The Central European Times Publishing Company asked for biographical data so as to include him in the *Who's Who Almanac 1934*.

1935
King Carol honoured him with the Order of Cultural Merit for Letters and Literary Works, Cavalier, Second Class.

1936
He was hospitalized in the psychiatric clinic of the Central Hospital of Bucharest.
Alcalay & Co Publishing House published *Comedii în fond* ('In Fact Comedies').
For the next ten years no new poems were published in any printed media.

1937
Many studies and essays referred to him as an outstanding poet of his generation.

1938
August Maria Holban translated into French a group of four poems and published them in the review *Viața Românească*.
Agatha Grigorescu-Bacovia who had been living in Bacău, now moved back to Bucharest to take up a teaching post there.

1939
Critics analyzed Bacovia's poetry, and declared him a literary descendent of Eminescu.

Mihail Jora, a well-known Romanian composer, published *Cântece pentru voce și pian* ('Songs for voice and piano') after poems by Tudor Arghezi and George Bacovia.

1941
The painter Coman Ardeleanu produced two portraits of the poet.

G. Calinescu synthesized the Bacovian poetic art in his famous *Istoria literaturii române de la origini până în prezent* ('A History of Romanian Literature from Its Origins to the Present').

1943
Fourteen of his poems were included in *Literatura română contemporană* ('Contemporary Romanian Literature') published by the Dacia Publishing House.

1944
July Bucharest was bombarded by American Air Forces. Agatha and Gabriel took refuge in Pucioasa. George remained in Bucharest.

October 28th Ovidiu Drimba mentioned the poet in his article *Creatori români de clasă universală* ('Romanian Creators of Universal Class') in *Tribuna română*, Bucharest.

November 5th Henry Jacquier translated into French an anthology of poems by Tudor Arghezi, Gheorge Bacovia, Ion Barbu and Lucian Blaga in *Națiunea Română*, Bucurest.

'Poems. Definitive Edition of Author' was published by the Royal Foundation.

1945
November 20th He was given a post as librarian at the Ministry for Mining and Oil.

1946
January 3rd He was promoted to Chief Librarian at the same Ministry.

April 1st His wages were doubled.

November 1st His 65th birthday and 50 years of literary activity were celebrated at the Ministry of Arts in a grand ceremony. He received an award of money.

November 28th The Ministry of Arts nominated him as their Cultural Councilor in the Department of Arts.

December 26th His fourth volume *Stanțe burgheze* ('Bourgeois Verses') was published by *Casa Școalelor Publishing House*.

He resumed an old hobby, drawing portraits, caricatures and other compositions. He also played the violin for which he was naturally gifted.

Chronology 15

1949–1954
The poet entered a shadow cone in public life, but within the family circle he was still active. He wrote over 60 poems, drew many portraits and caricatures. In this period he was under treatment for a long, ongoing lung disease.

1955
The Council of Ministers gave him an honorary pension.

1956
September He won 'Ordinul Muncii' ('Order of Work') first class.
December 14th His 75th birthday was celebrated.

1957
The poet agonized. In moments of lucidity he worked at a new volume of poems.
May 22nd 8.00 a.m. The poet George Bacovia died. Cause of death was given as Vesical Neoplasm.

1961
The Memorial House of George Bacovia was founded in Bucharest.

1971
Festivalul de poezie 'George Bacovia' (The 'George Bacovia' Poetry Festival) took place in Bacău.
His Memorial House in Bacău was inaugurated.

Translators' Notes

For me, the poetry of George Bacovia is in itself a sad 'doina', for it is full of music and longing. He longed for the women he loved who died before him; for a new social order for the poor so that their quality of life could be improved; and for a new self. Despite the fact that he had a good self-image about his writing that lasted to the end of his life, he was not positive regarding his personal appearance. He hated how he looked and the fact that he was always lonely, and imagined himself as set apart from the society into which he was born. In fact it was a self-imposed loneliness and solitude, that he also enjoyed. He was prone to nervous breakdowns and wrote about his 'madness' in many of his poems.

Bacovia was born in 1881, at a time when symbolism was in fashion in France, seen especially in the works of Rimbaud, Verlaine and Mallarmé, so that by 1916, when his first volume *PLUMB* appeared, he too was considered a symbolist poet. His poetry touched the public's imagination by evoking inexpressible subjective states, so much so that even today the 'person in the street' will say when asked, that they like Bacovia's poetry best because it expresses what they feel, deep down, about the state of their lives, past and present.

Personally, because I am a very positive person, I find this very sad, and as a translator it was hard to enter the poet's mind and feelings. However after a hard winter and a muddy, rainy season in Bucharest, where hospital care still leaves a lot to be desired and tuberculosis is again present in the society, I allowed myself to enter Bacovia's world and to experience vicariously his inner subjective state. The more we translated, the clearer the symbols became.

As you can see by the artwork we have included in this volume, Bacovia was a very good artist. He was also musical. He played the piano and the violin and his poems are full of references to songs, (the 'doina' in particular), chords, strings, arpeggios, harmonies, waltzes, brass bands, and orchestras. It is not surprising that his poems are written with an inner music and are heavily rhymed.

The Romanian language is one of the romance languages but has preserved a case system that suffixes the definite article. This together with the fact that spoken rhythms are notably iambic means that the language often rhymes quite naturally and so the music of poetry is intrinsic. Much of the vocabulary is Latin based but there have also been Slavonic, Greek and Turkish influences. Despite the presence of iambic pentamters, the natural rhymes can set a translator enormous problems. Fortunately Bacovia often wrote in a brief colloquial style, so I have taken the liberty to do this too, and where appropriate have inverted the syntax slightly where he placed words at the ends of lines so as to carry on the sense into the next idea. After all he was born at the time when Tennyson, Swinburne, D.G.Rossetti, Longfellow, R.W.Emerson, George Elliot, and Robert Browning were ending their lives, and, as with the French poets, their styles would still have been in fashion abroad for the next 50 years.

As a predecessor of Bacovia, Mihai Eminescu had selected and standardised the Romanian language just as Chaucer had standardised English, so Bacovia had a firm foundation on which to build. However from time to time, he tended to use old words that are not in current usage. On the whole his written style of language is simple and at times almost telegraphic, particularly in his later works. In fact in his 'Final Considerations' he refers to his own style as 'thrifty and concise'.

Another problem I found was the placing of the symbolic colours that Bacovia used for emphasis. In many cases it was essential to place them at the ends of lines to keep the foregrounding of the page, which for Bacovia is like writing music on manuscript paper. The chord has to come in a certain place or the atmosphere of the music is completely changed. To get over this I used a long hyphen before the word rather than adding 'so' or 'that is' as a prefix, while in the poem 'Pastel', as the colours referred to were funereal and worn for mourning, I used the word 'in', suggesting 'dressed in'.

His obsession with death and all things funereal dominate most of his poetry, but not his prose. In the short prose pieces, there are some delightful vignettes where he depicts children, and much to our surprise his prose poems include an erotic piece entitled 'The Black Cube'.

George Bacovia seemed condemned to wear a mask all his days, for he obviously lived a middle class life where he would have the opportunity to participate in many social events, such as attending balls. Half of him appears to have appreciated such beauty, while the other half criticises such events with a heavy sarcasm and bitterness. He spoke out for the 'underdog' and looked towards a 'new age of socialism.' The sad part is that when it came, although he still strongly believed in socialism, he began to realise that Communism was not the answer to all the problems. In his 'Final Considerations' (1954–57), which he dictated to his son, he states:

All scissors have a destiny: to spoil literary works.

Socialism is my friend. Let us have a drink in its honour, as at the lion's bridge.

Is the present dead? Has the future gone? Is the past coming to life? For whom?

Throughout his work, with only a few exceptions, sadness hangs over everything like a thick mist. If you were to analyse the vocabulary he uses, you would find that the most common words are to do with 'weeping' 'inner loneliness', 'wasteland', 'rain', 'blood', 'leaves', 'lead', 'twilight', 'autumn', 'wind', 'snow', 'yellow', 'violet', 'white', 'black', 'brass band funeral fanfares', 'death', 'wandering', and 'madness'. In symbolic terms, he impregnates the seasons with his strongest images that are 'death', 'sadness' and 'loneliness'. It was a period when tuberculosis (then known as consumption) was rife, and few survived it.

I hope this collection will be of help to those who wish to enter the world of Bacovia in order to rediscover his lonely inner trapped spirit, caught in contrasting worlds, that brought him despair and a deep well of sadness, forever brimming, like a tear ready to fall.

Brenda Walker
Bucharest 2005

* * * * *

Barbarous, was that woman's song,
Late, in the empty coffee bar
(Bacovia: 'Sad Evening' / *Seară tristă*)

Nothing can illustrate more clearly than the above lines, how remarkably concise and terse the poetry of George Bacovia can be. Not so long ago, another Romanian poet stated that Bacovia's poetry was so concentrated that it seared your tongue when you recited it. To translate Bacovia into a foreign language means to find those combinations of words that would enable you to preserve the same concentration.

From the point of view of the translator, Bacovia appears to be a creator who masters outstandingly well these three poetic tools: rhythm, rhyme and word.

The *rhythm* specific for each poem creates an unforgettable atmosphere of lamentation, or, quite rarely, exultation. I would rather say that his poems sound like incantations dedicated to the Gods of sadness, melancholy, solitude, neurosis, despair, longing, frustrated love, and so forth.

The *rhymes* that have the function of adhering the message to the reader's brain, are very striking, sometimes present with mathematical accuracy, that transform the images into obsessions.

Finally, the *words* are like musical quavers and/or brush strokes giving each line a melody or a visual image in nuances ranging from the dark: *Sleeping deep the coffins of lead / And flowers of lead and a funeral shroud* — . . . ('Lead'), to the ethereal: *Bud that's white and pink and pure, / Dream of sky and of azure,* . . . ('Spring Notes') or the philosophical: . . . *. And tell me why it's autumn / And why the leaves fall* . . . ('Pastel').

With so many challenges ahead, the conversion of Bacovia's poems into English was not an easy task. To our great luck, Brenda Walker is a remarkably gifted poet of great sensitivity, and puts the best of herself into everything she undertakes. This fact, combined with my lasting love for Bacovia's poetry, created a team which I feel has brought the English version as close as possible to the concentration of the Romanian text. If in English it does not sear the tongue, we hope at least it heats it a little.

Let the reader be the judge.

Stelian Apostolescu
Bucharest 2005

Bacovia, a Poet from the Edges of Existence

1. The poet — the person

When alive, Bacovia was considered a 'minor poet' and for a time after his death was quite forgotten. However today, he has again appeared on the scene, and is considered great. Within the Romanian cultural space on both sides of the River Prut, he has become an emblematic figure of the existential sensibility that in our dynamic and convulsive present, is consuming modern man with its stressful spiritual states. Bacovia is read and studied by high school and university students who discover themselves in the monotonous, melancholy tonality of his verses. Many books, studies, essays, and PhD theses are being written about his work, and the postmodernists consider him their forerunner due to his fragmentary style and deconstructivism.

How can you define a poet who once said that he was neither a traditionalist, nor a modernist, and could not be caged in any one trend or artistic movement? Nevertheless, in some interviews he did admit to being a 'poet of decadence'.

Above all, Bacovia was an isolate, immersed in a zone of darkness and an underworld of strange shadows, of phantoms in a melange of desperate shrieks, groans and a weeping that came from matter itself ('...*heard all matter weeping...*'). Such a solitary, timid figure, set apart by an endless neuroses, and living in a provincial environment so full of misery, he appears to have come straight out of the slums of Dickens, or the gallery of those unstable, lyrical characters of Tennyson. Within Emil Cioran's vision of despair and decomposition,

Bacovia seems a descendent of Shelley, for he penetrates 'into the innermost depth of our organism', into the visceral zone of the soul: 'The poet is an agent of destruction, a virus, an illness in disguise, much more dangerous, although miraculously uncertain for our red blood cells. To be around him means to feel your blood getting thinner, to dream of a paradise of anemia and to hear tears streaming through your veins . . . '

George Bacovia, christened Gheorghie Vasiliu, and the fifth child in the family, was born in Bacău on September 4th, 1881, at 2 p.m. His father was a grocer and his mother a clerk, while his grandfather was the sub-prefect of the county of Bacău. His pseudonym came from the Roman name for Bacău, which happened to be Bacovia, and was a name given to the greater part of the Moldavian region. The poet used to say that his pseudonym was composed from the abbreviation of *Bacchus*, the god of wine, and the word *via* that means 'way'. So his pen name meant 'The way of Bacchus'; a pertinent interpretation, for his native town was certainly surrounded by vineyards.

Bacovia always seemed to be governed by a demon of instability and dislocation, for he never concentrated enough to complete his university studies and avoided a social career. He preferred the humble job of public servant, seeming in this respect like a character from the prose of Chekov, Dickens, or Kafka. He would often leave jobs that had been offered to him, and after repeated attempts to settle in Bucharest or Iași, he eventually returned to his hometown of Bacău, where he stayed closeted away with his parents.

To return to his youth, with some interruptions he attended the Ferdinand High School in his native town and graduated in 1903. He left the Military School in Iași to enter the Faculty of Law at the University of Bucharest and eventually made great efforts to graduate. Finally he received his Law degree, but from the University of Iași, not Bucharest. He never practised this profession. Illness even prevented him from continuing his job of transcriber and assistant bookkeeper in the Bacău Prefect's office. In 1914, he was admitted to a mental sanatorium in Bucharest. At the beginning of the First World War he never took up his post as transcriber for the Department of Secondary Education at the Ministry of Education, due to the fact that he was evacuated to Iași, along with the archives. Illness again prevented him from remaining on the staff of the Ministry of Labour in Bucharest (1917-1920) and he returned to Bacău. His final job was that of substitute teacher for drawing and calligraphy at the Boys' School of Commerce in Bacău (from 1924 to 1928). Starting with the year 1928, he became director of the review, *Ateneul cultural*. His marriage to Agatha Grigorescu brought him back to Bucharest in 1928 where he launched the review, *Orizonturi noi* and for a while he was a Reader at the Department for People's Education. After retirement he still undertook the duties of a librarian for the Ministry for Mining and Oil (1945) and was also a consultant for the Ministry of Arts (1946).

As you can see, this poet belonged to the category of unadaptables, and those poets who seem forever cursed (poètes maudits).

His retreat into social anonymity and his determination to stay at the margins of public life in the shadow of humble jobs, did not however prevent him from distinguishing himself in the literary world. He benefited from the encouragement of the great poet Alexandru Macedonski, whom Bacovia valued as a 'classic poet, with a vast knowledge of Western and other cultures', and also as a 'poet of beauty and an olden times dreamer'. (In fact, in 1961, Macedonski wrote an epigram for Bacovia: '*You, dear poet, on your brow / Bear the laurel bough, / The only poet who, up till now / Has converted Lead into Gold.*')

The first volume *Plumb* 'Lead' (1916) was published with the help of poets Ion Pillat and N. Davidescu. The second publication, *Scântei galbene* 'Yellow Sparks' (1926), came about due to the insistence of the critic E. Lovinescu. In the year 1925, he was awarded the Prize of the Writers' Society, and in the year 1934, together with Tudor Arghezi, received the National Prize for Poetry. This recognition of his value developed over time, particularly after having published some new volumes from a compilation of poems written 'in breaks between working' and having as starting points what he called 'concrete elements' and 'biographical data': *Cu Voi* 'With You' (1930) *Comedii în fond* 'In Fact Comedies' (1936), *Stanțe burgheze* 'Bourgeois Verses' (1946), *Stanțe și versete* 'Verses and Poems' (in 1957, the year of his death).

Bacovia was permanently ill, a frail man who lived his life and wrote his poetry not as one with 'classic health', but with a 'romantic illness', which he expressed by means of 'symbolism'.

The sickly air, 'morbidezza', that dominates his poetry and prose with an air of authority, is not an expression of frustration, or of an eternally humiliated orphaned child. Nor is it a 'Cinderella complex'. It is merely the expression of indifference. He had the grey, anonymous existence of a lonely provincial, far away from the 'Centre of the world', who has arrived at an obscure periphery of it. Bacovia is pre-eminently the poet of that existential periphery, that shuts out all other perspectives and in full view, gives birth to a conscience of a fatal, tragic recluse.

By an artistic miracle combining staginess and artificiality with authenticity and naturalness, Bacovia converts 'pathology' into 'ontology'. His state of permanent illness helps him to better understand the innermost depths of his being, those hellish depths of his ego. It has been said that Bacovia is the only Romanian poet who descended into Hell.

This statement should be corrected, for Eminescu, the poet whom Bacovia so much admired, had descended there some time before. Bacovia's profound essence is very similar to that of Eminescu for he too possessed a true spirit. Considering a parallel with English poetry, one can find obvious affinities with the melancholy complexes of Tennyson based on contraries, and also with the 'spirit of loneliness' as expressed by Shelley. He can also be paralleled with the Pre-Raphaelites, and the 'aestheticism' and 'universal pain' of Keats in '*Ode on Melancholy*'.

2. Bacovia — the man within

Bacovia, poet of the 'existential periphery', was a loner, solitary and taciturn, tucked away in his parents' home in Bacău, 'inherited from fathers' forefathers'. An analogy that springs to mind is that of a snail, who emerges, shyly, from his house, with his gelatinous horns extremely sensitive toward anything happening in the outside world.

Bacovia's loneliness is not a social condition, it is a state of soul, accepted and lived as if were absolute reality. It is a state of many soul states, and dominant in the Bacovian psychic universe. Everything — impression, sensation, memories, sentiment, thought — is smelted into this overall state, which imposes its 'sovereignty' over his entire works. His unstable health that was forever with him, was only a conventional pretext; the confinement to a strictly limited circle of his loneliness had a metaphysical nature. It was lived with all the fibres of his being, like a fixed idea or an obsession. The condition itself demands of a poet such as Bacovia that he be solitary and temperamental, confined to a space of home-like loneliness. *And no one understands a thing — / I disappear to write in a tavern, / Or laugh and set off for home, / To confine myself as in a coffin.* ('Towards Autumn') His home, that acted as a shelter, totally suited the colour of melancholy that immersed this solitary man. He used to say: 'I usually stay at home most of the day, except for a few hours when I teach at school. I don't get bored or restless in my solitude. Due to my temperament, I've always wanted such a life. I have never been too healthy. Society always seeks out forceful men, who are successful in striving for it, pushing against all odds. They could never understand the melancholy of my being.'

One can also find a sensitive attitude towards the outside world, but the world is gazed at through the front window of his home. The noisy world is outside, full of 'spontaneous joy', over which the poet does not want to project the shadows of his deeply rooted sadness. 'Here, in provincial towns, life flows monotonously,' and contains, as in an embryo, the whole of life in a single day. The monotony that ends in total silence ('I prefer the silence') is converted into poetry with a monotonous style, tone, and atmosphere. His poems reveal 'landscapes of a soul': loneliness. Viewing Bacovia's poetry as a whole, one discovers it to be a self-recital, a song mumbled for himself alone, a musical 'mono-chord', without counterpoint. It is, to use postmodernist terms, an authorial discourse. Writing, as defined by the poet is communication with and within himself. It is an expression of his ego addressed not only to the reader, but also to the poet's own ego: 'I have no poetical creed. I write just as if I was talking to someone, because I like talking to them. Living so isolated, and not being able to communicate very well with other people, I often talk to myself, play music and, when I find something interesting, I take notes, and then later, recite them to myself. It is not my fault that these simple notes take on the shape of verses, and sometimes they even seem to be yelling. They were only meant for me.' (Given at an interview by I. Valerian in 1927).

As one can see, his poetry is an organic secretion, the spinning of the silken thread in the chrysalis. It is the song of the melancholy born from within himself, and the thought that springs from within thought itself.

The poet is tormented by a real obsession for colour, by 'painting with words' or, as he would say, 'a colourful rendition'. He loved the violin. 'For me, the melodies influence the way I think of colour. I play music and from the chords of the violin I write verses. Whether from scores, or from the ear of my soul, this instrument has been and still is my faithful friend. I even compose music, but it is only for myself.' As the painter uses colour, the poet tried to express colour in words: 'For each sentiment there is a corresponding colour. Now, lately I have been obsessed by yellow, the colour of despair. This is why I called my latest volume *Yellow Sparks*. In *Lead* Bacovia sees the colour yellow, which is in fact specific to lead's chemical compounds and consonant to his temperament. Burnt lead is yellow, and so is the burnt soul. 'In my test tube,' says the poet, 'any chemical reaction ends up with a yellow precipitate.' The impression of colour produced by lead is static and suggests the weight of a downward pressure. 'The greatest pressure of lead is on humans. How would you feel in a vault of lead?' And the poet cites from his poem: '*Sleeping deep the coffins of lead,/ And flowers of lead and the funeral shroud — / I stood alone in the vault ... and a wind stirred ... / And rasping were the wreaths of lead. // Turned in sleep my lover of lead/ On flowers of lead ... and I began to call-/ I stood alone near the body ... and felt the chill ... / And drooping were its wings of lead.*' ('Lead')

White and black are funereal colours: '*Trees in white, trees in black/ Stand in the lonely park, bare:/ Mourning décor, a funeral bier ... /Trees in white, trees in black.// In the park once more regrets fill the air . . . //With feathers in white, feathers in black, / A bird who bitterly chatters/ Throughout the old park wanders/ With feathers in white, feathers in black. // In the park the ghosts appear //...*' ('Décor')

Violet is universally used by symbolists to suggest twilight. It places everything in the realm of decomposition, of nothingness, of falling into a state without will power, of somnolence and a substance-less uniformity: the autumn twilight is violet, *'the whole crowd seems violet', 'the whole town is violet'* ('Violet Twilight'), *'Daybreak of violet'* ('One Morning'), the Spring has *'vibrations of violet'* ('Springtime Nerves'), Venus is a lively violet, horizons are violet, the mill wheel is violet, the lancet is violet ('One Morning'), the cemetery is violet ('Twilight') and so on.

The violet that is 'par excellence' the colour of neurosis and morbidity, has definitely conquered the poet's soul since he has an acute conscience of the non-being having installed itself authoritatively in the universe.

3. Modern Man — Archaic Man

Studied attentively, the Bacovian man proves to be always full of surprises: he lives only in the area of paradox: de-concerning, upsetting, astonishing others with his protean stature. He appears to repeat the same gestures, intimating a behaviour that seems both common and monotonous, a retroaction into the shell of his ego. It is a permanent retirement into the pure biological depths, accompanied by a specific existential vibration. The path that leads to this state would appear to be simply Freudian from the moment of frustration to that of repression. However, the Bacovian man certainly does not remain the small man in a 'small century': "*In this world's circle banal and greedy . . . / A cry greatly convulses me deep down; / And this way (of being) will be till doom/ And nothing in this world, startles me.* ('Vobiscum') Thus, the way of being for the poet is eternal; the world being looked upon as 'sub specie aeternitatis', for he himself is 'convulsed' by a 'cry . . . deep down'.

Bacovian man is not simply *'the lone one of deserted squares'*, the common solitary being. He is the eternal solitary figure, propelled by his own internal weeping into the weeping of matter, or vice versa (there is no essential difference). Is there a purely romantic conflict with 'this world's circle banal and greedy', analogous to Eminescu's 'narrow circle'? Or are we dealing here with a glacial, distant, indifferent eternity? The frequent invocation from the infinite, the presence of cemeteries, of snow, of rain — that bring even the echoes of universal cosmic weeping — , the leaden sky and the flowing leaves all seem to suggest a grandiose eternity, cold and aloof. Bacovia's modern dimension consists of irritation, a state of excitement, fear, trembling, spasms; in a word — *morbidezza*, often augmented with satanic overtones. Such a familiarity with eternity has a titanic-negativist feeling about it.

However, another kind of eternity exists for Bacovia. It is one of the archetypal aurora-like beginnings of the world. The movement towards 'eternal rest' and 'severe eternity', mentioned in the poem 'Perhaps Tomorrow', towards frozen star-ways where he wanders in the 'terrible night' towards the infinite, is mentioned again and again with a 'Come', or even with a 'Howl' ('— *Come* . . . / — *Come* . . . / -*To the infinite*'; '*Howl . . . Howl . . . far off under frozen starways . . . / In the terrible night whose door shall I knock on?* 'Winter's Lead'). This is correlated with a movement *illo tempore* toward the primordial elements of the world. The secret axis of Bacovianism is the violent impact when modern man meets archaic man. Enduring the terror of history, the first has nerves (of Autumn, of Winter, of Spring, and even of Summer, the last coming from 'the heat of the day'), while the second intercepts this terror with serenity, suggesting an eternal rebirth. The acute feeling of *sameness*, lived profoundly by the 'Bacovian being' is disconcerting and frustrating while at the same time, liberating and fulfilling. The meaningful principle of the antinomy, the reciprocal challenge and the enforcement of contraries is fully developed, putting in dialectic balance that which is empty and that which is full: *There are moments when I have it all . . . / Silent, sweet psychoses — / Lovely tales like dreams of roses . . . / There are times when I have it all . . . // See, there are moments when I have it all . . . / Life is spent with words in a row — / A song from the past . . . long ago . . . /There are times when I have it all . . .* ('In Happiness')

These paradoxical *'moments when I have it all'*, 'fix only the moment of *hybris* (here of 'happiness')', when the fullness brings about the emptiness, realizing it, making it more dreadful and more markedly affected by the non-being.

The retirement, the acts of confinement, of running away from reality, typical for the Bacovian man, reveal something of his link to archaic man, for he was also a seeker of secure dwellings and archetypal domains.

The poetry of the Idea suggests how the Bacovian ego loses itself in a dialogue with Eternity, with Shadows, between normality and temptation. In Bacovia's poems, archaic man and modern man mimic and challenge each other, bringing about a strange symbiosis, yet a natural one along the line of genuinely-satanic Bacovianism. Why? Because modern man belongs to history, while archaic man belongs to prehistory or protohistory; the first is anchored in actuality and caught by it, while the second avoids it, boycotting it by re-living and re-starting the beginning of the world.

According to Mircea Eliade, the dialogue between the above two men, would have had reason for reciprocal reproach. Modern man, who can be creative only if he is part of history and finds his inspiration in his own freedom. This freedom to make history by realizing himself would rebuke archaic man for the fact that he cannot create as long as he is a prisoner of habit, repeating ad infinitum the first free gestures of mankind. Or, is it possible for modern man to make history by himself while history is being made either by itself, or by a reduced number of people, or even by just one man? 'Thus, for the traditional man, modern man offers neither the type of free being, nor that of a creator of history. On the contrary, the man of archaic civilizations can be proud of his mode of existence that enables him to be more than he was, free to annihilate his own "history" by periodical abolition of time and collective regeneration. This freedom with regard to his own "history" — which for modern man is only irreversible, yet constitutes human existence — cannot be indulged by the man who wants to be historical' (Mircea Eliade, *Essays*, Bucharest, 1991, p. 115).

The Bacovian man is endowed with 'the freedom to realize history by realizing himself,' suggesting the flowing, the collapse, the sliding into nowhere, confinement inside the proper circle, the aspirations flown away on the wind, the solar apparition of some joys of Spring, the universal creation of 'lead, tempest, wasteland'. All these contribute to a perpetual sense of termination, and an annihilating end. It is a history that is being made under the sign of 'the misunderstood' and in the void of individual solitude.

Another obvious quality of Bacovian man is that of being able to regenerate time, to make it cyclical, unhistorical or trans-historical, in other words, eternal. He is at liberty to believe he is the same as before: *Alas, it's the hour of years gone by, wet shadows are crossing, / And in the draft of a passageway full of rainwater, I doze.* ('Nocturne'). The Bacovian night is pre-genesis: within it all possibilities germinate. '*The call from the depths of the earth*' from 'Melancholy' is an invitation to familiarize oneself with the breeze of eternity. The Bacovian Spring is full of regenerating possibilities. It does not break the spell of the dream, but rather stimulates it. To rediscover the proper powers during and due to Spring, is an act characteristic to traditional man. *Green and new, green and new . . . / Bud that's white and pink and pure, / I still see you, I still hear you,/ Dream of sky and of azure /.* ('Springtime Notes')

However, the main characteristic of the Bacovian man — again in the spirit of the archaic man — is that of effectively transcending time by a gesture of spontaneous abolition, either by a bizarre mixture of rain and snow: *And autumn and winter / Descend together; /And shower and snow — /And snow and shower.* ('Sleet'), or an elementary iteration of *the same* leading automatically to other times or *illo tempore*, or by enforcing and universalizing feelings: . . . *Heard all matter weeping* ('Lake Dwellings'). Time is transcended also by projecting the sadness: *And there slowly, calmer, / They gather around sighing — / Yearning for 'tomorrow', their sister, / Yearning for my being.* ('Days Pass'), or the unabated thirst for the Absolute, an idea expressed by Eminescu, meeting the infinite cold of the sky, as in 'Sometimes': . . . *And I'll take from the sky / What I no longer / Find among the stars, / Since I began to wander. / I prefer to think like this / When I yearn eagerly — / Or the sky is cold / To infinity . . .* Modern man, caught by neuroses, morbidity and the '*yearning for tomorrow*', goes to the flowing bed of history toward an uncertain finish, but belonging also to eternity, while archaic man, serene and confident, comes from the archetypal past, re-living human existence from the beginning when he met his first love, first fear and first nerves. The eternal return is captured in the poem aptly entitled 'Memento': *And while the snowstorm wanders . . . / The hours of the clock have rasped / The sufferings of dead souls — / Though . . . these are things of the past // And while the snowstorm wanders . . . /Once again, loves that were lost / Awaken lonely poets — / Though . . . these are things from the past! // And while the snowstorm wanders . . . / As on an unknown coast . . . / Once more I think that you are lovely — / Though . . . these are things of the past!.*

4. The Existential Emptiness

In the life of the psyche, as was shown by Stephane Lupasco, a French Philosopher of Romanian origin, there are two factors that activate and enforce each other. On the one hand there is the identical and homogenous, while on the other there is the non-identical and heterogeneous. To realise life, forces the possibility of death while to realise death, creates the possibility for life. 'Focusing on life, our conscience is populated with death, focusing on death, it is populated with life' (Stephane Lupasco, *Psychic Universe*, Iași, 2000, p. 126). Poets strongly manifest a consciousness of death. The psychologist Pierre Janet considers that even for a normal person the idea of death is a morbid phenomenon. Caught in this process of focusing on life and death, the conscience oscillates between homogeneity and heterogeneity and knows two kinds of morbid manifestation: *schizophrenic* (when it fixes in homogenous and enforces the heterogeneous) and *maniac-depressive* (when it fixes on heterogeneous and enforces the homogenous).

The actual malady, the pathologic state is conditioned by the abolition of the conflict that paralyzes the development of the dialectics: 'Any actual malady is the absence of conflict among the cellular and cerebral levels. The sick man is the man who abandons the fight, or else the fight abandons him' (op. cit. P. 224).

Bacovia suspends any conflict between life and death; more than that: he perceives life as if it is a death. Death appears itself without being referred to life. Everywhere — in the manifestations of nature, on the faces of people, (his sweetheart included), and in their behaviour, in the insignificant daily happenings, in the various aspects of the sky — the poet perceives the signs of degeneration, of disjointment, of dissociation, in a single word, 'nothingness'.

His poetry has the character of a funeral ritual with liturgical incantations. There is a funeral march, a Biblical wailing (of Job), a stifled mourning with a cosmic resonance, which sometimes ends in a desperate shout, with an exclamation: *Listen how it rains / How depressing!* ('Rarely'); *Oh. Dream . . . Oh, freedom . . . / Howl! Howl! . . . far off under frozen star-ways.* ('Winter's Lead'); *Oh, keening of bells when it rains!* ('It's Raining'); *Oh, when will there be different spring-time arias?* ('Springtime Nerves'); *How rapidly it snows, how rapidly!* ('About Winter'); *High School — cemetery / Of all my youthful days!* ('High School'); *Flowers on horizons, in the grass — flowers . . . / Jesus!* ('Hymn'); *I said to myself: It is late - / Oh, thoughts, / In the world!* ('When Alone'); *Inside my heart there's autumn!* ('And All').

When such exclamations are absent, there appear the meditative questions or short conclusive formulae like: *And again all are sad, / Today as yesterday.* ('Piano'); *Nothing now remains.* ('Gaudeamus'); *Relative, / Pardon.* ('Ideas'); *A famous / Aphorism / Helps you / To live . . . / It is neither tomorrow, / Nor today, / Nor yesterday — / The time . . .* ('Cogito').

Bacovia is like a tragic Narcissus, who sees in the mirror his own face which he identifies with the face of death. He is a Narcissus who, marked by this implacable identification is immobilized only in his melancholy, obsessive thoughts. Under the terror of such dark thoughts, in which one can hear the fluttering of the wings of Poe's raven, he opens a one-man theatre where he plays out his destiny: does mechanical gestures, laughs sarcastically, *senselessly*, ('Autumn Nerves'), invoking also the sarcastic laughs of those who seem kin to his ideas:

Poe, Baudelaire and Rollinat ('Finis'), cries with *tremble as in a frenzy* ('Pulvis'), stages movements of a loner, gets 'irritated', invents dramas of the hospital and dramas of rape ('In the Park'); he lies back as if dying /*Spreading roses on myself, faded-jaded flowers*/ ('Poem in the Mirror'); weeps softly, full of alcohol and beaten by rain, like a skeleton, he knocks at his sweetheart's window with a coin ('Autumn Nerves'); passes nervously *from one room to the other / On the strike of the satanic hour.* ('Midnight'); walks *palid and silent* on a street among *Thousands of women* and caught by melancholy ('Springtime Notes'); mimics the death of King Romulus ('Tempest').

One should mention the décors for they are nocturnal, autumnal, crepuscular, with clavier wailing, with 'humid wind' with military brass bands: *What a sad opera playing*, with red, yellow and green ghosts, with phantom-like beings as in the *Hysteria of humans, / Beneath the wailing ravens* ('About Winter'), with mourning waltzes and funeral marches, with sad darkness, with *Leaden grass and strong air* ('Autumn Nerves'), *with pain and with mystery* ('A Tale'), with deaf silences, with tremors and *icy rains* ('Morning'), with perfume of wet roses and homely sigh ('Love Song'), with infernal rains.

It is a 'theatrum mundi', staged by a satanic Demiurge and dominated by the terror of the Nothing. The Bacovian ego, fully theatrical, initiates a senseless game, the game of the Absurd itself.

There appears the tragic theatrical performance of a Nothing invading the stage coming from everywhere: from the lights of the day, from nocturnal silences, from telluric depths or from the glory of the sky. The spirit of Nihilation haunts a world in which the disease of degradation is at work. From the hollow sphere of the Cosmos one hears the sounds of a universal insanity: *Immensity, eternity, / You, chaos, gathering all the same . . . / In your emptiness is insanity — / And you make us all insane.* ('Dust'). All that is material, all that has sense is swallowed up by this void of Nothing which is a true cosmic black hole.

The lovers are overtaken by the night, since *All day nothing has happened* ('Sic Transit II'); and from the sounds of the past centuries there remains only the Nothing between them and the poet who appears an unsure horizon and metaphysical threshold so that: *Let your mind linger in Non-being / Buzzing through the centuries, / There is nothing more to retain / Of the many things once murmured. // There isn't and never was; / Day after day has rolled. / An unsure horizon, / And metaphysical threshold.* ('Sine Die')

On this musical wave of Non-being sounds dematerialize, slide into other sounds, more stifled, more obscure.

The critic Ion Negoitescu once stated: 'If with Mallarmé the technical artifice creates for itself the motivation for delight, being just the narcissism of a virtuoso, with Bacovia, technique is the slave to his emotional states, overwhelming by their pitiful misery, states of failure and the banal, so far from the Mallarmean orchestral ethers. The Bacovian rhythms are more complicated, getting more and more obscure through lack of images, the inner music of the ideas shrink until disfigurement, from where another music starts, undecipherable and tragic.' (*Istoria literaturii romane*, vol I, Bucharest, 1991, p. 268). The Bacovian sadness being total and the fingerprint of disorder so profound, the ultra-fine musical technique is reabsorbed in an exclamation, in a yell.

George Bacovia, who combines in an incredible way the spontaneous, novel, native sensation with the technical artifice, with the irrational (mystery, strangeness, sliding in 'nerves', funereal ritual, melancholy of the late and of the too-late) and with the rational (the 'clear' metaphysical projections of the cosmos, of the nothingness, of the archaic, the conceptual revaluation of colours), the poetic with the counter-poetic, performs a singular figure among the symbolists and avangardists, surpassing them due to the existential core and the obscure inner music, 'undecipherable and outrunning postmodernism'.

Bacovia is the Brancussi of Poetry. Like the author of 'The Column without End, 'The Bird in Flight' and 'The Table of Silence', the author of *Lead*, of *Yellow Sparks* and *In Fact Comedies* is a 'bowl of essences', a searcher for Fibonacci's Gold Section. Both of them are in some way 'primitives', 'carvers' of ideas of essential symbolic forms. (Brancussi was interested not in the bird as such, but in the idea of flight).

'I gave to my poems the luminaries of joy' wrote Bacovia in a Brancussian spirit, in *Useful Digressions*. Joy and Bacovia? Yes! The joy of sincerity, the joy of expressing with theatrical tricks, the joy of re-discovering the pristine peace, the silence of thinking: *Bacovia, / The country / Where any thought / Is silent*... ('Stanza for Bacovia')

The deep meaning of life is found in the fatal passing *From the loneliness / Of life / Into the loneliness / Of death*... ('Loneliness, I didn't Want You'). Nevertheless, at the end of the poem there appears the eulogy of life: *Poets, avoid / Loneliness. / Among people / There's life*...

As a symbolist, an anti-symbolist, a decadent with the light from the beginning of the world and from resurrection (the flowers on horizons invoke Jesus in 'Hymn'), an expressionist who censors pathos with humor, an existentialist by nature, Bacovia either concentrates his visions in stanzas and verses, in a very grudging vocabulary in the style of a 'doina', (a love song and elegy), or else he melts them into an inner musical fluid. What we have left is an exemplary poet of essences.

Mihai Cimpoi
Chișinău
May 2004

Lead

Plumb, 1916

Lead (*Plumb*) together with the original Romanian version / 39
Pastel (*Pastel* 'Buciumă toamna . . .') / 40
Décor (*Decor*) / 41
Twilight (*Amurg* 'Trec corbii — ah, "Corbii . . ."') / 42
A Lake-Dwelling (*Lacustră*) / 43
Grey (*Gri*) / 44
Sonnet (*Sonet*) / 45
Autumn Twilight (*Amurg de toamnă*) / 46
A Picture of Winter (*Tablou de iarnă*) / 47
In the Garden (*În grădină*) / 48
Near Autumn (*Spre toamnă*) / 49
Paling (*Pălind*) / 50
Violet Twilight (*Amurg violet*) / 51
December (*Decembre*) / 52
Black (*Negru*) / 53
Neurosis (*Nevrosă*) / 54
Sleet (*Moină*) / 55
Melancholy (*Melancolie*) / 56
Rarely (*Rar*) / 57
Autumn Nerves (*Nervi de toamnă* 'E toamnă, e foșnet . . .') / 58
Sad Evening (*Seară tristă*) / 59
Autumn Notes (*Note de toamnă* 'Tăcere . . . e toamnă în cetate . . .') / 60
Oh, Twilights (*Oh, amurguri*) / 61
Winter Twilight (*Amurg de iarnă*) / 62
Yearning (*Alean*) / 63
Ancient Twilgiht (*Amurg antic*) / 64

Dust (*Pulvis*) / 65
July (*Cuptor*) / 66
Autumn (*Toamnă* 'Răsună din margini de târg . . .') / 67
Lonely (*Singur*) / 68
Exhausted (*Trudit*) / 69
Twilight (*Amurg* 'Ca lacrimi mari de sânge . . .') / 70
Otherwise (*Altfel*) / 71
Peepshow (*Panoramă*) / 72
Finis (*Finis*) / 73
Winter's Lead (*Plumb de iarnă*
    'Iarna, de-o vreme, mă duce regretul . . .') / 74
Nocturne (*Nocturnă* 'Stau . . . și moina cade, apă, glod . . .') / 75
Autumn Lead (*Plumb de toamnă*) / 76
Largo (*Largo*) / 77
It's Raining (*Plouă*) / 78
Springtime Nerves (*Nervi de primăvară*
    'Primăvară . . . O pictură parfumată . . .') / 79
One Morning (*Matinală*) / 80
In the Park (*În parc*) / 81
Poem in the Mirror (*Poemă în oglindă*) / 82
White (*Alb*) / 84
Autumn Nerves (*Nervi de toamnă*
    'La toamnă, când frunza va îngălbeni . . .') / 85
Winter's Lead (*Plumb de iarnă*
    'Ninge secular, tăcere, pare a fi bine . . .') / 86
Autumn Notes (*Note de toamnă*
    'Toamna-n grădină și-acordă vioara . . .') / 87
Monosyllables of Autumn (*Monosilab de toamnă*) / 88
Nocturne (*Nocturnă* 'Uitarea venea . . . a venit . . .') / 89

Lead *Plumb*

Sleeping deep the coffins of lead,
And flowers of lead and the funeral shroud —
I stood alone in the vault . . . and a wind stirred . . .
And rasping were the wreaths of lead.

Turned in sleep my lover of lead
On flowers of lead . . . and I began to call —
I stood alone near the body . . . and felt the chill . . .
And drooping were its wings of lead.

Plumb

Dormeau adânc sicriele de plumb,
Și flori de plumb și funerar vestmânt —
Stam singur în cavou . . . și era vânt...
Și scârțâiau coroanele de plumb.

Dormeau întors amorul meu de plumb
Pe flori de plumb . . . și-am început să-l strig —
Stam singur lângă mort . . . și era frig . . .
Și-i atârnau aripile de plumb.

Pastel *Pastel*

The horn of autumn
Agonizes — beyond —
Birds flutter by
And secretly abscond.

Rain drizzles . . .
Not a soul about;
If you stay outside
Smoke will get your throat.

Far off, in the fields,
Unhurried, ravens fall;
And long lows
Come from the stall.

Sad cow bells
Ring out hoarse . . .
And it's getting late
And I'm not yet a corpse . . .

Décor   *Decor*

Trees in white, trees in black,
Stand in the lonely park, bare:
Mourning décor, a funeral bier . . .
Trees in white, trees in black.

In the park once more regrets fill the air . . .

With feathers in white, feathers in black,
A bird who bitterly chatters
Throughout the old park wanders . . .
With feathers in white, feathers in black.

In the park the ghosts appear . . .

And leaves in white, leaves in black;
Trees in white, trees in black;
With feathers in white, feathers in black,
Mourning décor, a funeral bier . . .

In the park the snow falls slower . . .

Twilight *Amurg*

Ravens fly — ah, 'The Ravens'
Of the poet Tradem —
Flowing to bed down
Over an icy town,

They go on wastelands . . .
While, from silver,
In a twilight of silver
A new crescent is lit

On silver horizons
In the vast vault . . .
My love . . . ah, 'The Ravens'
Of the poet Tradem . . .

A Lake-Dwelling *Lacustră*

So many nights I hear it raining,
Hear all matter weeping . . .
I'm alone, and my thoughts cling
To stilt dwellings on the lake.

I seem asleep on wet planks,
A wave slaps me hard on the back —
I shudder in sleep, for I think
I left the brig on the bank.

A void of history stretches before me,
I find myself there in time . . .
And sense how with so much rain
The grey suports have tumbled down.

So many nights I hear it raining,
Everything shuddering, everything waiting . . .
I'm alone, and my thoughts cling
To the dwellings on the lake . . .

Grey   *Gri*

At open windows ill omen weeps all day,
And the leaden world of winter is landing;
'Can you hear the ravens?' — I asked myself . . . sobbing;
While on the heavy leaden horizon
                    It snows *grey.*

As on the horizon, my thoughts to blackness stray . . .
And in the world I grow more alone, more barbarous, —
Sad, it's with a feather I sweep the hearth, a recluse . . .
While on the heavy leaden horizon
                    It snows *grey.*

Sonnet *Sonet*

It's a wet night, heavy, outside you'd drown.
Through the fog — tired, red, no sky line —
Sad, smoking, street lamps shine,
As in a steamy, dirty tavern in the town.

In the slums the night seems blacker . . .
Streams in sad houses are flooding —
And one hears a dry, bitter coughing —
Through old walls ready to founder.

Like Edgar Poe, I'm going back home,
Or like Verlaine, fired with drink —
And tonight I don't care a damn I'm alone.

Then, pacing steps that must look amusing,
In darkness I grope around my home,
Fall, re-fall, and never stop talking.

Autumn Twilight   *Amurg de toamnă*

Twilight of autumn, of clay, no one there,
On the field ominous whispers pass on the wind —
Far off poplars bow and flail to the ground
In great lazy seesaws, of rubber.

A deep emptiness . . . with head on the pillow,
I hear the sighing of my dead lover;
I listen carefully staring in mid-air,
And sigh, cry, and laugh, with a ha, and a ho . . .

A Picture of Winter   *Tablou de iarnă*

It snows heavily on the field to the slaughter-house
And warm blood streams in the furrow;
The blood of animals soaks the snow —
It never stops snowing on sad skating ice . . .

The white is kindled by blood now curdled,
And the ravens step through gore . . . and gulp;
But the hour is late . . . above, ravens skulk
On the field to the slaughter house night has unfurled.

It never stops snowing on the skybed's floor . . .
And now when sad windows are kindling
Wolves come to the slaughter-house — twinkling.
— My darling, it's me at the frozen door . . .

In the Garden   În grădină

Autumn creaks from tired, worn out limbs
In ancient fences, in the wooden tiles' decline
And leaves fall like some sinister sign
In the stillness of a garden when it quietens.

A pale maiden with hurried motions
Is waiting for her new lover . . .
While, discordant and sinister
Autumn creaks from tired, worn out limbs

Near Autumn *Spre toamnă*

On streets in a frenzy,
When autumn's come,
A thought follows me
Wills me on:

— Pass away, and hurry!

When I reach my lover's house,
Nervously, I force the window down,
And call for her to see how the foliage
Is raining on the rainy town.

But look, there's a Jewish funeral . . .
And it rains, there's sleet, sludge —
In strange Semitic mumbles
I too join the cortège.

And no one understands anything —
I disappear to write in a tavern,
Or laugh and set off for home,
To confine myself as in a coffin.

As always in a frenzy
When autumn's come,
A thought drowses me
Wills me on:

— Pass away, and hurry!

Paling *Pălind*

I'm the lone one of deserted squares
With sad bulbs with pale light —
When copper rings out in the black night
I'm the lone one of deserted squares.

My friend is a hideous laugh, with a shadow
That scares off dogs roaming around drains;
Under sad bulbs with pale rays,
My friend is a hideous laugh, with a shadow.

I'm the lone one of deserted squares
With games of shadows that bring on madness;
Paling in silence and with paralysis —
I'm the lone one of deserted squares . . .

Violet Twilight   *Amurg violet*

    Twilight of autumn, violet . . .
Further off, two poplars seem silhouettes:
— Apostles in garments of violets —
    The whole town is violet.

    Twilight of autumn, violet . . .
On the street a lazy world, a coquette;
The whole crowd seems violet,
    The whole town is violet.

    Twilight of autumn, violet . . .
From tower, from field, Voivodes' helmets;
Forefathers pass in clusters of violets,
    The whole town is violet.

December   *Decembre*

Look how December is snowing...
Through the window, look darling —
Tell them to bring in the logs
So we hear the busy fire crackling.

And lead the armchair to the flame,
To the chimney to hear the gale,
Or my days — they're both the same —
I'd like to learn their musical tale.

And tell them to bring in the tea,
And then come closer, my dearest —
Read me something from the North Pole,
And let it snow... drifts to bury us.

How warm it is here by you,
Look how December is snowing —
And everything here so holy...
Don't laugh... go on reading.

It's daytime and yet how dark...
And ask them for a lamp or candle —
Look, the snow is up to the fence,
And frost has covered the door handle.

I cannot set out for home today...
To go back or go on I'll meet drifting,
See how December is snowing...
Don't laugh... still go on reading.

Black   *Negru*

Incinerated flowers, boundless black . . .
Black, burnt, coffins of metal,
Shrouds of charcoal for the funeral,
Deep black, boundless black . . .

Jangled sparks of dreams . . . boundless black;
Incinerated, love steamed —
Scent of burnt feathers and it rained . . .
Black, only boundless black . . .

Neurosis   *Nevrosă*

Outside snow is ravaging,
My love touches the keyboard —
And all the town is in darkness,
As if it's snowing in a graveyard.

My love plays a funeral march,
But I wonder, puzzling hard:
Why she plays a funeral march . . .
While it snows as in a graveyard.

She weeps and leans heavily on the keys,
Sighing loudly as if fevered . . .
The piano dies in discord,
While it snows as in a graveyard.

And I weep too, and trembling
Lift her tresses from the keyboard . . .
Outside the town's deserted,
While it snows as in a graveyard.

Sleet *Moină*

And autumn and winter
Descend together;
And shower and snow —
And snow and shower.

And night is falling
Empty and foul;
And jaundiced sick pass
Children from the school.

And walls are damp,
And a cold's coming on me —
With those in the cemetery
A thought never leaves me . . .

And autumn and winter
Descend together,
And shower and snow —
And snow and shower.

Melancholy   *Melancolie*

What a howl, what moans of autumn . . .
And the forest, rumbles wildly —
A horn resounds in the gorges,
And the *doina is starting more sadly.

— Now listen well, my darling,
Don't cry and don't be terrified —
Listen how gravely from the depths
The earth calls us to his side . . .

* *A doina is a sad Romanian song of longing*

Rarely *Rar*

Alone, alone, alone,
In an inn, far away —
The innkeeper also sleeps,
The streets are empty today.
Alone, alone, alone . . .

It rains, it rains, it rains,
Time now for drinking —
To hear how my soul weeps,
How depressing!
It rains, it rains, it rains . . .

No one, no one, no one,
It's all for the best —
And for some time
No one knows where I rest
No one, no one, no one . . .

Tremble, tremble, tremble . . .
Any irony
Is reserved for you —
The night grows elderly.
Tremble, tremble, tremble . . .

For ever, ever, ever,
All wanderings, it seems,
From now will never call me —
Hoarfrost covers dreams.
Forever, ever, ever . . .

Alone, alone, alone . . .
Time now for drinking —
Listen how it rains,
How depressing!
Alone, alone, alone . . .

Autumn Nerves *Nervi de toamnă*

It's autumn, it's rustle, it's sleep . . .
The trees on the street, gasp in pain;
It's coughing, it's mourning; it's bare . . .
      And it's cold, with a fine rain.

Lovers, much sicker, much sadder,
On their way make gestures that seem odd —
And leaves in eternal sleep,
      Fall heavily, waterlogged.

I stay, and I go, and I return,
And lovers deepen my sadness again —
I start laughing senselessly,
      And it's cold, with a fine rain.

Sad Evening   *Seară tristă*

Barbarous, was that woman's song,
Late, in the empty café bar,
Barbarous the song, yet full of sorrow —
And all around was such uproar . . .
And in the blaring noise of the piano
Barbarous was that woman's song.

Barbarous, was that woman's song,
Amid cigarette smoke like clouds,
We were a sad gatheing of fellows —
Pondering non-existent worlds . . .
While in long, satanic echoes,
Barbarous, was that woman's song.

Barbarous, was that woman's song,
And all around was such uproar . . .
And we no longer left for our homes,
And we cried with heads on our arms,
While above us in the empty bar,
Barbarous, was that woman's song . . .

Autumn Notes   *Note de toamnă*

Silence . . . in the citadel it's autumn . . .
It rains . . . and only the rain has words —
It is a leaden peace, a wind, and on the winds
Leaves pass hurriedly to freedom.

Open up, let me in — adored one,
I come with boughs and leaves that have dried;
In town, a sad poor girl has died —
And they buried her, and in the rain they've gone . . .

Let me in, in the citadel it's autumn —
The whole land seems like a tomb . . .
Rain . . . and in the town led by the wind,
Leaves pass hurriedly to freedom.

Oh, Twilights *Oh, amurguri*

Oh, twilights of violet . . .

It's coming —
Winter, with the piccolos' plaintive keening . . .

Over the abandoned park
Falls regretting
And a croak, black, stark . . .

Eternity,
Cares . . .
From funeral fanfares
Autumn tolls, agony . . .

An icy wind is ready for off,
And under the skeleton gibbet —
A wild, deranged laugh.

Of you, no sign, nothing,
— Coming, not coming . . .

Oh, twilights of violet . . .

Winter Twilight *Amurg de iarnă*

Winter twilight, funereal, of metal
The white field — an immense round —
Rowing, a raven comes slowly from beyond,
Cutting the skyline at a diagonal.

The trees, rare and snowy, seem crystal.
The calls of loss absorb me,
While the same raven returns silently,
Cutting the skyline at a diagonal.

Yearning *Alean*

It's dawn, a chill of autumn,
And there as you gaze
Are coiling wisps of smoke,
And across orchards — a haze.

Resounding, sad voices,
Of empty fields and lanes —
And heavy blows and yells
Are heard from hillside vines.

With a kite children run,
At the child in you, you gaze,
And you weep . . . in a chill of autumn . . .
And across orchards — a haze.

Ancient Twilgiht *Amurg antic*

The fountain behind the dead palace
Still flows, still rains, tears flood —
And drops falling at twilight, take on shades:
Of sea-blue, of gold, of blood.

A line of white swans is sailing,
The lake reflects the park's dreamy mood —
The twilight coats the swans in shades:
Of sea-blue, of gold, of blood.

Forgotten, all the white statues gaze out,
Dreaming, white, in the air tears flood —
And the twilight casts on them shades:
Of sea-blue, of gold, of blood.

Dust *Pulvis*

Immensity, eternity,
You, chaos, gathering all the same . . .
In your emptiness is insanity —
And you make us all insane.

In front of you I cower down.
Immensity, eternity —
I love a girl that's from the town . . .
Teach me philosophy.

Immensity, eternity,
While I tremble as in a frenzy,
With what supreme irony
You point behind to a cemetery.

July *Cuptor*

There are a few dead in the town, my love,
That's what I came to tell you today;
On the bier, from the heat of the town —
Slowly, the corpses are rotting away.

The living move, yet are also rotting,
Their clay steaming from the heat;
It smells of corpses, my love,
And today even your breasts wilt.

Bring perfumes to cover the mats,
Gather roses for on you they'll stay;
There are a few dead in the town, my love,
And slowly, the corpses are rotting away . . .

Autumn *Toamnă*

Resounding from the edge of town
A gunshot powerfully cracks;
It's autumn . . . metallic the sound
Of trumpeters, behind the barracks.

One hears a school bell ringing,
It's windy, and deserted, it's morning;
Papers and leaves, in many piles,
Set off round the square, spinning.

The Cathedral watches the horizon,
From its spire, majestic and stern;
The town gardens are keening,
Flinging greenery to the town.

And there sounds as in ancient times,
From borders, a bugle alarm for attacks;
It's autumn . . . metallic the sound
Of trumpeters, behind the barracks.

Lonely *Singur*

In a deluge fall white stars of crystal,
And it snows on this night when sins are stirring
At the hearth — with the flame hardly flickering —
Today, even my last dream died like a mortal.

And it snows in a midnight that's glacial . . .
And you shiver again, my lonely soul —
On the hearth — with weak flame, glowing coal —
Fall slowly, pink tears of crystal.

Exhausted   *Trudit*

My love, again I am here . . .
Though today I'm not feeling so well —
Open the piano and play for me
The old death knell.

And should I fall to the floor
In the sad and silent room —
Keep on playing, my love.
Slowly, the same tune.

Twilight   *Amurg*

Like great tears of blood
Leaves from the boughs flow —
And blood-red, the twilight
Slowly penetrates the window.

Over the hills of blue,
Like blood, the moon's ascending,
Like blood is the lake,
Forever it is reddening.

In the sick twilight a girl
Coughs at the window;
And has made her 'kerchief
Like the leaves that flow.

Otherwise *Altfel*

The man had started talking to himself . . .
And everything moved as shadows passed on —
A leaden sky set to rule forever,
But the brain burned like a flame fom the sun.

Nothing. The emptiness seemed even wider . . .
And in its bitter night all songs were silent —
And with his mind now livid, and brow bent,
The man had started talking to himself . . .

Peepshow *Panoramă*

It wept that hurdy-gurdy-fanfare
Dismally in the night, late on . . .
And alone, I peered down the lenses,
Lost in the empty museum . . .

And in the world of sad lenses
I was gripped by sinister ideas —
Around me were wax figures,
With fixed and hideous leers.

And that hurdy-gurdy-fanfare
Unlatched a satanic shiver;
In glass coffins — princesses
Breathed, mechanically, in organza.

And then I fled full of dread
From the gloomy, lurid museum,
The town slept on in silence,
Hollowly wept the barrel-organ.

It wept the hurdy-gurdy-fanfare
A sad aria, lost to memory . . .
I stood petrified . . . as the citadel seemed
Cursed, century after century.

Finis *Finis*

The body laid out on the bier in splendour,
Under rays of silver dreams in the vast room . . .
While lost in the gala of death was her bosom —
Halted forever, breathtaking in splendour.

A wasteland . . .

Far off, in the citadel of clattering life . . .
Oh, how my feelings were boiling over . . .
But in the dismal room hoots of sarcastic laughter
From Poe, and Baudelaire, and Rollinat.

Winter's Lead   *Plumb de iarnă*

Lately, this winter, I've been led by regret
Through copses, by the sides of railways —
I go alone at twilight by frozen-waterways,
While fluttering over the world, that violet.

The paleness, the muteness, mimic my heart
Under a new crescent, over snowed up villages;
I go alone across solitary, metal bridges,
And wait in the snow . . . but for what?

Howl! . . . Howl! . . . far off under frozen-starways . . .
In the terrible night whose door will I knock on? . . .
Oh, dream . . . Oh, freedom . . .
Howl! Howl! . . . far off under frozen-starways.

Nocturne *Nocturnă*

I'm here . . . and sleet falls, water, mire . . .
To know nothing again, there's one way clear —
A lamp agonizes, it's here, not here —
A drunk crosses the sad square.

The town, wet from heavy dampness, sleeps.
Behind these walls, perhaps she too sleeps,
Iron money houses in brick houses,
And the heavy gate closes.

A piano above softly sends an echo.
Like sad luggage in mud stands my shadow —
Drops splash,
Grime snows in the town,
From a window, in a glass,
A yellow rose peers down.

Autumn Lead *Plumb de toamnă*

Already, a girl has died from coughing,
A pale dreamer kills himself with a gun;
It's autumn and now night has fallen . . .
— And my forgotten love, how are you faring?

In the public gardens, at rest,
I heard a madman roaring,
And in swarms leaves are escaping;
It's windy and everywhere hope is lost.

In the town, poverty without end,
I met a soldier, a parson . . .
From now I'll sleep on books, forgotten,
Lost in a provincial wasteland.

Already echoes of revolt and sorrowing
Have begun in these mistaken times;
Do you still read about social problems . . .
Or, my forgotten love, are you still writing?

Largo   *Largo*

The music sonorized every atom . . .
Longing for you and for another kingdom,
Longing . . .
To hover
Pain without a name . . .
Over man . . .
Everyone finds himself pondering,
On life — how it's vanishing.
The music sentimentalized.
Languishing —
Longing for you and for another kingdom,
Longing . . .
The music sonorized every atom . . .

It's Raining   *Plouă*

Yes, I've never seen such rain . . .
And the heavy cattle bell, sleepy, dire,
How it tolls in the old byre!
How it tolls in my mute soul again!

Oh, the keening of bells when it rains!

And what thought is always nagging!
What a primeval day of mire!
A sick girl, a neighbour
In the rain, roars laughing . . .

Oh, the keening of bells when it rains!

Yes, it's raining . . . tolling meek and mild
Like all that's love or hate —
And sad music from a flute
Comes from a nearby — child.

Oh, the keening of bells when it rains!

What tales bells tell over again!
What a world so empty of dreams!
. . . And how can you not weep in chasms,
Yes, how can you not die insane.

Oh, the keening of bells when it rains!

Springtime Nerves   *Nervi de primăvară*

Spring's in the air . . .
A perfumed painting with vibrations of violet.
In shop windows, verses by a new poet;
In town a waltz sighing in a fanfare.

A new springtime of dreams and ideas . . .

An endless awakening is buzzed once more,
It's clear with just the sun.
At a factory window starting at the horizon
Is a pale-faced woman staring at the azure.

A new springtime over old fears . . .

On the never-ending field again peasants appear,
In the infinite, the earth seems to quiver:
Now there'll be plenty as before, and forever,
But there again it's just a never-ending idea.

Oh, when will there be different spring-time arias?

One Morning   *Matinală*

Daybreak of violet
Raining coloured dew —
Venus, quivering anew,
Seems a living violet.

I tap slowly at your lancet
I tap with a rose, blood-red —
Come on flower, sleepy-head,
While the sky is violet.

Waters weep drop by droplet,
And everything still sleeps —
As in dreams the mill wheel keeps
Growing a deeper — violet.

Bare the posy of your breast
Bare flower, sleepy-head . . .
Sad, with the rose, blood-red,
I tap the violet lancet.

Daybreak of violet
Staining with colour —
Venus, quivering paler,
Seems a snuffed violet.

In the Park *În parc*

Now the park stands ravaged, it's fatal,
Rusted by cancer and wasting away,
Stained red, live prey —
Now, one spins the drama of the hospital.

Then, she could joke,
Flapping wings of euphoria;
Perfume, pollen and hysteria —
Then, she too came to the park.

Now in an empty park blooded leaves drape
White statues of women;
White models of fine dimension,
Now one spins the drama of rape . . .

Poem in the Mirror *Poemă în oglindă*

In the living-room full of dreams,
In the wide-oval mirror with the silver frame,
Strikes autumn
And the gangrened garden,
In the wide-oval mirror with the silver frame.

In the armchair, weary, in ample folds of silk,
While violet is falling,
You read, intoning
A decadent poem, perfumed cadaverously,
Monotonously.

I foresee the pink poem of future love . . .

But absent-minded with sick eyes,
You thieve, ironically, the perfumed room's surroundings,
And your gaze cascades vaguely over the wide-oval water,
Over the gangrened garden,
Over autumn in the mirror —
Lulled asleep . . .

I foresee the pink poem of future love.

But pale, I'm now entering the ravaged garden
And on the abandoned table — white sculptured marble —
Clothed in mourning,
I lie back as if dying,
Spreading roses on myself, faded-jaded flowers
Just like us . . .

Let the final melody be spoken by the dusted piano,
Or is autumn's weeping from the fountain-night enough.
You see from the old armchair —

Lead

The agony of violet,
The bier,
And the gangrened garden,
In the wide-oval mirror with the silver frame . . .

White *Alb*

The orchestra began with gracious indignation.
The white ballroom dreamed of roses — white ones —
A waltz of veils — white ones . . .
Infinite space, of a harmonious lamentation . . .

In the dawn full of violins,
The white dancers scattered on unforgotten traces —
Singing bright kisses . . .
Vast, a miniature of future times . . .

Autumn Nerves   *Nervi de toamnă*

In autumn, when the leaves are yellowing,
When those with T.B. have surprises coming —
Addicted, as I've never been before, rain beaten,
Late on, I'll tap slowly at your window with a coin.

And in this wet autumn, more rotten than those passed away,
When the wind wails again, for those up or down in clay —
At your window, in the terror of night, like a long finale,
I'll say again that years pass more arduously, more brutally.

The rain will fall . . . and I'll be crying at your window, late . . .
A drunken skeleton wandering, around in the night —
And you'll hear nothing of anything I wanted to say . . .
In this wet autumn, more rotten than those passed away.

Winter's Lead   *Plumb de iarnă*

Age-old in silence, appearing to be fine, it snows,
Through the white town, only the wind doesn't hasten —
It snows, all seem to have died, all seem to have risen . . .

Scholarly tomes sleep in iced shop windows.

Between walls, on distant spires,
It snows with nothing in the vast night, they snow banknotes —
Only the lonely wind weeps other notes . . .

My shadow wears itself away in democratic districts.

In the vast town as never before it snows grandly.
Social dramas snow at cinemas,
While in glacial boulevards the wind guffaws . . .

— But who could possibly explain this sad story ?

Autumn Notes *Note de toamnă*

Autumn in the garden tunes its violin,
The street is deserted . . .
The town is full of grain silos —
For the new bread the droning mills begin.

A leaf has settled on a stretched hand, begging . . .

The empty town . . .
A remote citadel;
Greenery gouged . . .
For electric cables, paralyzing it,
Like a symbol,
A bird drops in the town — yet one more sadness.

And night comes . . . and silence is falling . . .

A lost boatman, my mind will drown,
On times' course —
And from the sorrow of no longer penning a verse . . .

I am the saddest person in this town.

Monosyllables of Autumn   *Monosilab de toamnă*

Autumn tolls the glass with leaves of metal,
                            Wind.
Within the heavy silence, thought and animal,
                            Weak.

In the room, sadly the wood tolls mute:
                            Split.
Shadows left about in an empty, silent,
                            Spot.

In vain, I alone, with a quill on the sheets
                            Scratch.
The lamp weeps . . . your years, my years
                            Stretch.

I could stay in bed, my eyes closed, still
                            Will.
Very soon, slowly into a void they'll all
                            Fall.

Oh, sometime there'll be another, natural
                            Stream.
Autumn tolls the glass with leaves of metal,
                            Dream.

Nocturne *Nocturnă*

Forgetting it was coming ... it came.
A tear trickles down, all is silence
The tired lamp blinks again,
Any touched object whispers: leave me in peace ...

From now on ...
Rain weeping on the street, listen,
On a deep uproar,
On the print of a small shoe in a park long before ...

Asleep ... listen ...
Outside, at the window, autumn said:
— Ah!

Yellow Sparks
Scântei galbene, 1926

Yellow Sparks (*Scântei galbene*
    'O femeie în doliu pe stradă...') / 93
Alone (*Singur* 'Odaia mea mă înspăimântă...') / 94
Twilight (*Amurg* 'Crai-nou verde pal...') / 95
Midnight (*Miezul nopții*) / 96
Wind (*Vânt*) / 97
Echo of a Serenade (*Ecou de serenadă*) / 98
A Night (*Noapte*) / 99
Phantoms (*Strigoii*) / 100
Funeral March (*Marș funebru*) / 101
Ballet (*Balet*) / 103
The Worker's Serenade (*Serenada muncitorului*) / 104
Pastel (*Pastel* 'Adio, pică frunza...') / 105
Yellow Sparks (*Scântei galbene*
    'Vom spune că toamna a venit...') / 106
Dozing (*Dormitând*) / 107
Nocturne (*Nocturnă* 'E-o muzică de toamnă...') / 108
Springtime Nerves (*Nervi de primăvară*
    'Melancolia m-a prins pe stradă...') / 109
Springtime Notes (*Note de primăvară*) / 110
Summer Twilight (*Amurg de vară*) / 111
Fanfare (*Fanfară*) / 112
Emptiness (*Gol*) / 113
Nocturne (*Nocturnă* 'Clar de noapte parfumat...') / 114
About Winter (*De iarnă* 'Cum ninge repede...') / 115
The Shadow (*Umbra*) / 116

About Winter (*De iarnă* 'În ecouri bocitoare . . .') / 117
To a Maiden (*Unei fecioare*) / 118
Autumn Notes (*Note de toamnă* 'În toamnă violetă . . .') / 119
Autumn Waltz (*Vals de toamnă*) / 120
Nocturne (*Nocturnă* 'O, nu mai cânta . . .') / 121
It's Snowing (*Ninge* 'Când iar începe . . .') / 122
Hygiene (*Igienă*) / 123
And it's Snowing. . . (*Și ninge* . . .) / 124
Winter's Lead (*Plumb de iarnă* 'Și iar . . .') / 125
Autumn Nerves (*Nervi de toamnă*
    'Iarbă de plumb și aer tare . . .') / 126
Autumn (*Toamnă* 'Clavirile plâng în oraș . . .') / 127
Nocturne (*Nocturnă* 'Nu e nimeni . . . plouă . . .') / 128
A Tale (*Poveste*) / 129
Among Walls (*Între ziduri*) / 130
Cold (*Frig*) / 131
Morning (*Dimineață*) / 132
Love Song (*Romanță* 'Parfumul rozelor ude . . .') / 133

Yellow Sparks *Scântei galbene*

A woman clad in mourning on a road,
A yellow leaf quivered after her —
Carried away by the town's feud,
I had forgotten autumn would be here.

Long ago there was a road,
A school, and a frost falling —
In classrooms, quite unnoticed,
A lonely pupil was paling.

A man, at twilight, on a road . . .
Who knows how he trod leaves there —
Under the tramping, and the world's load . . .
— I had forgotten autumn would be here.

Alone *Singur*

My room terrifies me
Painted with black stripes —
Unbraided autumn, on thousands of pipes,
Plays at night, unceasingly.

— Oh, room, full of mysteries,
In your peace a madness lies;
Black shadows sleep in all the crannies,
On the table a flame shies.

— Oh, room, full of echoes,
When tears start to ensnare,
The black paintings' sadness shows —
The flame trembles in the mirror.

My room terrifies me . . .
Here not even a lover should tarry —
Unbraided autumn, on thousands of pipes,
Plays at night unceasingly.

Twilight *Amurg*

New pale green crescent and lonely me
Among the boughs rattling like skeletons —
Purple like a dead body . . .
— Come to the violet aspens.

Or maybe not! The lights of the town kindle . . .
Other people, and another bard —
It's been long since we slept with shadows
In the violet graveyard . . .

Midnight *Miezul nopții*

The greenery has now begun
A slothful, sorrowful hora*;
But I weep, and with the crying night
The willow outside seems my sister.

Very slowly midnight approaches
And one hears the leaves' *hora —
I go from one room to the other
On the strike of the satanic hour.

* *The Hora is a Romanian round dance*

Wind   *Vânt*

Autumn cried out with a sad accent,
The glance falls absent,
The wind resounds in the panels,
A cooper beating empty barrels.

Near the door the leaves are gathering,
From afar come old echoes of weeping,
Frost, a literary autumn,
On the streets dust prepares for action.

And I stayed alone much annoyed
By the riverside decadence,
And among tangled boughs jotted
Verses with no talent or sense.

Echo of Serenade *Ecou de serenadă*

Black pansies, velvety
On white marble have faded away
And, in sacred notes have frittered away
Sad perfumes, dolefully.

I alone with the shadow have again arrived,
Oh, statues, sad and shabby —
Black pansies, velvety,
Dreams, ah, dreams, here they died.

In clothes, black and gloomy,
I weep in the park long since abandoned . . .
And my serenade's lost to the wind,
In clumsy notes, and a cursed medley . . .

A Night   *Noapte*

Boulevards stretch at night in summer,
Electricity lights up a tree —
At the station an engine breaks free
And in the emptiness, train signals quiver.

In the sapphire sky, misers' treasure . . .
Silence uselessly vibrates with rumour —
The town, very slowly, seems but a room —
Where now, deep asleep, virgins quiver.

Phantoms *Strigoii*

With red lanterns, yellow ones, and green
Phantoms trek through fields of wheat
And dogs bark at the fields all night —
Phantoms go to the tavern, the garret,
And the garret can be seen bizarrely lit
With red lanterns, yellow ones, and green.

The phantoms return for what once was theirs,
Pawned when alive, left from yesteryear . . .
So the tale goes, I can't quite remember it,
At night, in the tavern, silhouettes appear
With red lanterns, yellow ones, and green.

But when the cock crows at first light,
They burst from the garret, troupes of phantoms,
In a chasm over the crops, the phantoms are lost
                        Red, yellow and green.

Funeral March *Marș funebru*

It snowed richly, and sadly it snowed; and it was late
When in the street, at a window, a chord stopped me;
And I wept at the window, and a frenzy captured me —
Bitter across the night the wind whistled, desolate.

Through the curtains I saw a large and bare room,
There at a piano, a brunette was playing,
Her hair falling into a cloak of mourning,
And she played sadly, moaning between flames.

The louring march composed by Chopin
Was repeated with mad gusto . . .
And the funeral melody rang out from the window,
While the wind whistled like the scream of a train.

Then, a blonde girl entered the room . . .
And almost naked, half-asleep, joined in
Taking from the piano a blackened violin —
And played, lost in the monotonous tune.

Tall, unbraided, white as lime water,
She seemed to me Ophelia demented . . .
And the bow with a long moan played
The dreaded louring march, a funeral air.

The piece was bitter, a crescendo,
The sad piano wept, as well as the violin —
The flames' trembled the light again,
The piano seemed a bier, and not a piano.

Later, the piano died, a long moaning,
The flames struggled in agony . . .

And slowly there spread a night of eternity,
And lastly, I heard a body falling heavily.

Alas, since then the world seems sadder.
Life is a melody like a funeral air . . .
And I'll never forget the demented fiddler —
And the sad, transfigured, piano player.

Ballet *Balet*

The gliding ballerinas — white . . .
Set free from a strict mould,
White before an enormous world
The gliding ballerinas — white . . .

The gliding ballerinas — white
And the world breathes, passions loosed —
White, they smile at a world seduced,
The gliding ballerinas — white.

The gliding ballerinas — white . . .
Secretly they wake organic weakness —
White, they stir satanic tendencies,
The gliding ballerinas — white.

The Worker's Serenade *Serenada muncitorului*

To you I'm just another monster
Hatching a longing for a new era,
And in your world — not much space . . .
But soon I'll clout it on the face.

Oh, always sleep deep, to revel
In sweet, hideous, bourgeois dreams,
Sighing, if I build you mansions,
I know how to demolish them as well.

To night, look, listen to him croon
A serenade, rough, turgid,
For lovers lost beneath the moon,
Poets with a love that's putrid.

Oh, stay asleep in endless night,
Bourgeoisie with triumphal airs,
Still prehistoric creatures
In the golden age of light.

None should weep under a pale moon,
But all revenge should quickly fade,
For all the martyrs bathed in blood,
I sing this very last serenade.

Oh, sleep . . . I'll go to the sun, climbing
In the sublime flight of aeroplanes . . .
With sweet, bourgeois, tyrannical dreams:
That's an aurora I find appalling . . .

Pastel *Pastel*

— Adieu, the leaf falls
And is yellowing like you —
You stay, and cry no more,
And forget about us two.

And my lover has gone
And is lost in the horizon —
And I call out foolishly
In the emptiness of autumn.

— Keep on being winsome
With your hands so small,
And tell me why it's autumn
And why leaves fall . . .

Yellow Sparks *Scântei galbene*

Let's say that autumn came . . . very sadly —
At a melancholy window something seemed near,
Yet a voice woke me, philosophically . . .
Damp wind and leaf fly somewhere.

Then I found myself near water in a field . . .
At the edge, a well-known poet meditating —
It seemed he had no place in this world;
And I was so sorry that this was happening.

I know nothing more, and I set out for home,
Look now how bare, what a ruin in night's glow —
The yellow twilight's yellowed me, weighs me down
Like yellow windowpanes, with tears that no longer flow.

Dozing *Dormitând*

In the haze of winter nights, when chimneys are smoking,
When lamps on the streets, in their thousands are watching,
Into the coloured haze I merge, hardly sensed —
I feel that I've made mistakes, much more than the rest.
I have been so lonely, and lonely I remain.
A merciless chit-chat weeps within my brain . . .

From beyond snowy walls there's music from a dance,
I linger, and there weeps in me — a provincial waltz.
From the snowy window with its finely draped curtains,
I go down icy streets within their swarm of stars;
And in the middle of my room alone I make a bow:
— In white with silver shoes, a blonde is waltzing now . . .

Kindling the lamp on the table, again I get undressed,
I'd like to make some tea, but can't, I just need rest . . .
I totter towards the bed as if never to sleep again —
A merciless chit-chat weeps within my brain . . .

Nocturne *Nocturnă*

It is the music of autumn
With the voice of a piccolo,
With the flute's sweet quavers,
With the tone of a violin.

And chords from keyboards
Lost in the sordino;
And everything's a funeral march
Through the night, sighs flow . . .

Springtime Nerves *Nervi de primăvară*

Melancholy has caught me on the street,
I am befuddled.
Oh, springtime, has returned . . .
Pallid and silent . . .
Thousands of women have passed;
Melancholy has caught me on the street.

It's a vibration of violets;
She passes too;
I'd have liked to —
But greet her I couldn't;
Oh, and how she passed,
In a vibration of violets!

Nothingness caught me on the street;
I was benumbed.
Oh, springtime has returned
Pale and forgotten . . .
A funeral waltz, here then gone.
Melancholy keeps me on the street . . .

Springtime Notes   *Note de primăvară*

Green and new, green and new . . .
Bud that's white and pink and pure,
Dream of sky and of azure,
I still see you, still hear you!

Oh, mark with your flame,
Sunshine, sunshine . . .
My body that bears such pain,
Due to Time's game.

From a willow comes a whistling,
Spring,
At a well a young girl, tarrying
Starts mimicking
On the open clearing . . .

Green and new, green and new . . .
Bud that's white and pink and pure,
I still see you, still hear you,
Dream of sky and of azure.

Summer Twilight *Amurg de vară*

Hysterical pale virgins
At open windows, fluttery . . .
In red, nuptial twilights,
Stand pale, and no longer marry.

I pass by, grown old, as they have,
And like them my heart rends . . .
Passing by each of them, I leave
A rose of blood in the curtains.

Fanfare *Fanfară*

What a sad opera playing
A military fanfare
Late at night, in the gardens...
And all the town grieving,
A military fanfare.

I wept and wandered on the street
In the night — vast, clear skylands;
And then empty was the street —
But the lovers filled the gardens.

The town lit by electricity
Gave out tremors of madness —
It was a night in September,
So cold and a wilderness!

And all the town grieving
A military fanfare...
Late at night, in the gardens
What a sad opera playing
A military fanfare.

Emptiness *Gol*

All the tiny leaves rustle,
The shade is cool in the sonorous copse —
A silent wonder, maybe brutal,
A dizziness of autumn, of a round dance.

A chaos wants to come with me
To forget the unique, and the number —
A dry rustling dries me,
I weep against a tree as on a shoulder.

And there twitters a light rain
On precipices, on the dried pine —
The cave from an ancient time . . .
And the darkened sky-line . . .

Nocturne *Nocturnă*

Night-light so full of scent,
A garden with its horizon so distant . . .
And asleep, on the old bench, reason argues unreasoning,
The cricket notches up the night, with nothing.

How I've been waiting . . .
Everything's flown —
The moon seems, when sighing,
To be a continent, well-known.

Here everything's set out so well
Every spike;
The centuries have stood still
A town, in a valley — a Keepsake.

Night-light so full of scent,
A garden with its horizon so distant . . .
And asleep on the old bench, ever shrinking . . .
The cricket notches up the night, with nothing . . .

About Winter   *De iarnă*

How fast it snows, then slowly,
And there's no telling how long it will last,
At the window — white,
A girl with a black shawl in the snowy porch . . .

But through the wide trees the night sets in —
In a snowy distance nothing's changed.
That's the truth
And bells jingle nightly,
Somewhere there's bound to be a dance,
Or a spiritualist séance
There's so much to do . . .

When it seems you're just a memory,
How rapidly it snows, how rapidly!

The Shadow   *Umbra*

Time dusted me while sleeping over pages . . .
The abyss from which you cannot leave, stretches;
A shadow, in the room, on my shoulders. I felt it lean —
It kept speaking the unspoken, I kept seeing the unseen.

— You may go to bed, the hour and night grow elderly,
You will write, something, sometime, or else nothing,
You're but a shadow now, and in my arms you're rising,
Leaving the lamp smoked and the room empty . . .

About Winter *De iarnă*

In lamenting echoes
Winter's coming, within minutes —
Infants cry at doors
In wheedling harmonies.

Virgins cry at pianos
Behind boyars' facades —
Harmonies cry at windows
Beggars from cemeteries.

Blindly come the rioters
And the hungry ones kill —
From villages to the town
Peasants have sent — ravens.

In towns of the well-provided
Hysteria of humans,
Beneath the wailer ravens
Women pass absent-minded.

Look, it's snows, unusually so —
Come to the hearth, to the stories —
Harmonies cry at windows
Beggars from cemeteries.

To a Maiden   *Unei fecioare*

The maiden is an avid reader;
Plays the piano, can paint and sew —
And has lain awake for nights in a row,
And perhaps that's why she's thinner.

Everyone thinks, and some have said —
But don't tell, it's a secret —
The young lady dreams of a poet,
Bizarre, lonely, gone in the head.

Autumn Notes *Note de toamnă*

In the violet autumn, famous composers
Arranged a great concert . . .
On yellow alleys sad poets recite long poems —
As always, it's an autumn when everything moans,
Beautiful, and inert.

On elegant streets, like a notion,
The modern woman has now found herself;
All chaos is a frivolity of the ether.
And, if the town goes into a convulsion
And the brain remains lost;
And, if work is creaking from arms, from stone, from iron ore —
The anonymous crowd should be given consideration.
All that I need, I can ask for . . .

Perfume . . . lit bulbs and violet arson
Flicker the twilight over the town's glass and pelf —
Lost in thought, I too leave, with defeated arms,
Weeping,
And humming,
Thinking only of myself.

Autumn Waltz   *Vals de toamnă*

Autumn plays at windows, funereally,
A mournful waltz, always the same . . .
— Come and waltz, my love, around the room,
To autumn's dirge for the mortuary.

Listen how the music resounds clearly
In the splendid park, solemn and old —
With plaintive wooden instruments, cold
Autumn plays at windows, funereally.

Now the waltz sighs, and slows right down,
Oh, now let me hold you close to me . . .
— Come and waltz, my love, crazily
To autumn's dirge for the mortuary.

Nocturne *Nocturnă*

Oh, stop playing you vagrant harmonies,
Just because I'm crying and don't know where I'm going,
In an autumn that laments ancient modesties.
With the rain that flows in slow, slum miseries,
Tonight when thoughts are so confusing.
Oh, it's raining, and your tears moan in harmonies . . .
— Always reminding others of my being . . .
Oh, stop playing you vagrant harmonies,
Just because I'm crying and don't know where I'm going.

It's Snowing *Ninge*

When it starts to snow again
I feel a longing embrace me,
I see myself far away, snowed in
On a road, walking slowly.

Under the eaves, the verandah
Is sadly growing darker;
A girl stays leaning
Against a snowy pillar.

Hygiene *Igienă*

She thinks I am contagious . . .
And is afraid when I kiss her,
But she sighs, a slave to pleasure,
And asks for a longer kiss.

At last, when the spasms cease,
She wets her kerchief with scent —
And puts it on her mouth, despondent,
Wiping away a consumptive kiss.

And It's Snowing... *Şi ninge...*

And in the large town, it's snowing,
It's a night full of revellry,
Again at balls, gold glittery
Orchestras and fanfares are playing.

Ladies of the night, at kerb edges
Waylay you as they wait alone,
Debauchery of beer and wine
In bars and coffee houses.

With the shop windows dazzling
With diamonds and with rubies . . .
And the town is packed with riches,
And in the large town it's snowing!

Winter's Lead *Plumb de iarnă*

And again ... the same hour every morning ...
The same secret smouldering on everyone;
A violet cold, and the face comes into being —
— Oh, look how concrete man has become ...

Long boredoms in the sombre towers ...
With a dry guffaw, late on, a sea of superstitions;
— You will deserve a lamp in downcast shadows
And from nights of waste you will fling out ravens.

In the stormy night, if you manage to overthrow
A sad indulgence or a secret whim —
They shall hear in towers, shall watch it snow ...
— Oh, look how concrete man has become ...

Autumn Nerves *Nervi de toamnă*

Leaden grass and strong air . . .
An eczema hoeing my face under powder;
On the field with a shadow of an idea —
Violet, ravens and mirrors of water.

— Oh, you who will wander like me
In dark colours, with a staggering gait —
Lured by something better, by beauty . . .
Long ago, during autumn, a voice was blown out.

Autumn   *Toamnă*

Pianos are weeping in town . . .

Outside, a time of lead
And the wind scatters the rain,
Autumnal leaves rush along
Fleeing the town streets in a swarm.

A sick poet, infected,
Pauses coughing near windows —
A girl behind a lattice is weeping,
Stares as the moon does through boughs.

She weeps . . . he is palid, and wasting
In this town, that's wild and dour;
And it seems that this picture,
Like an antique, is full of enigma!

Nocturne *Nocturnă*

No-one about . . . it's raining . . . a baby owl is crying
On a stone roof in the night with the torrent's echoes,
Alas, it's the hour of years gone by, wet shadows are crossing,
And in the draft of a passageway full of rainwater, I doze.

The plates of the drainpipes make all sound insane . . .
A hasty alchemy like flares fluttering,
Alas, it's the hour of years gone by, wrinkles of rain are crossing,
A stone town asleep . . . all are in pain.

No-one about . . . it's raining . . . a baby owl is crying.

A Tale *Poveste*

Do you recall the day when I said you were beautiful,
When with blood-red lips and sparkling eyes
Under the autumn trees you used to stop, bashful,
Turning our minds towards the love we felt so many times?
You wanted me to be the poet more daring than ever,
To hear the cool echo of some warm kisses,
You were moving towards a shadow much darker
Like a pale dizziness descending from other worlds.
Ah, you told me simply that you thirsted for loving.
Listening only to the lonely wood's whisper,
Your hand was on your breast and your eyes were smiling,
The pain of our separation you could stand no longer.
— Ha, ha, ha, the echo laughed and we laughed at your ecstasy.
Between man and woman you placed hate from days gone by.
I let you tell me the story with pain and with mystery
And I listened like an unknown passer-by.

Do you recall the day when I said you were beautiful,
When, among the wood's whispers, perhaps I kissed you
Listening to the cool echo, towards the autumn chill
Bringing to our meeting a distant adieu?

Among Walls *Între ziduri*

As I pass by large houses . . . looking for no one
                                                    in particular . . .
Oh, autumn of sleepy rustlings, let your whispers help
                                                    me slumber . . .
Onto the empty street, the winds suddenly pelt,
Silence reigns under arches and courtyards of asphalt

Everything's just as glorious . . . but never at peace . . .
Oh, autumn of long rustlings, let your whispers teach
                                                  me silence . . .
Oh, it's nothing, nothing, it was a great dream I felt.
Silence reigns under arches and courtyards of asphalt.

Cold *Frig*

I'm near a fence that's rotted,
And the wind blows wet leaves on lanes —
I'm uglier, I'm emaciated,
The cold begins to blur the panes.

The street slopes down to the valley
It's an autumn like an ancient poem —
The wind swells women's skirts as they journey,
But I could never pair up with any of them.

The autumn tears at bill boards and flowers,
It's sadder further off in the ravines —
And many times daily you make up the fires;
Oh, one has to be sad far off in the ravines . . .

A flake of snow wanders . . .

Morning   *Dimineață*

A black coffee . . . and an icy rain coming,
When the mind still burns with colours the room knows —
A quick look at a book, on with clothes,
And my steps lead me right into the morning.

As the cold, oscillating like a rumour,
Still complains of what's mine, what's yours . . .
Still I remain with what is left over,
And it rains as if evil were the cause.

I forgot I was walking . . . that I still like what's 'me' . . .
I got there in time, and then sat down.
But thoughts lie heavy with the weight of a stone . . .
I can no longer talk . . . I can only see . . .

Love Song   *Romanță*

The scent of wet roses,
Autumnal sighs,
Calls you, imposes
At dawn, during silent cries.

A sad poem of a leaf
Tells the story of our grief . . .
— Adieu, loneliness and pleasure.
Perhaps once we'll be together . . .

With You

Cu Voi, 1930

With You (*Cu voi*) / 137
High School (*Liceu*) / 138
Prose (*Proză* 'Amorul, hidos ca un satir . . .') / 139
Crises (*Crize*) / 140
Prose (*Proză* 'Plouă . . .') / 141
Bountiful (*Belșug*) / 142
Ego (*Ego*) / 143
The Shoes (*Pantofii*) / 144
A Storm (*Furtună*) / 145
Twilight (*Amurg* 'Pe seară, la geamuri,
    un nor violet . . .') / 146
Hymn (*Imn*) / 147
Winter Dialogue (*Dialog de iarnă*) / 148
Nocturne (*Nocturnă* 'Fug rătăcind în noaptea cetății . . .') / 150
Somewhere Else (*Aiurea*) / 151
Psalm (*Psalm*) / 152
Contrast (*Contrast*) / 153
A Ballad (*Baladă* 'O noapte de sineală . . .') / 154
Vobiscum (*Vobiscum*) / 155
Twilight (*Amurg* 'Trec burgheze colorate . . .') / 156
Piano (*Piano*) / 157
Mystery (*Mister*) / 158
Vae Soli (*Vae soli*) / 159
At the Altar (*În altar*) / 160
The Final Poem (*Poemă finală*) / 161
Violated Sepulcres (*Sepulcre violate*) / 162

Epitaph (*Epitaf*) / 163
Enough (*Destul*) / 164
On the Hill (*Pe deal*) / 165
At the End (*Din urmă*) / 166

With You   *Cu voi*

Much better lonely and forgotten,
Lost to relive it all again in a stupor,
In this country full of humour,
Much better lonely and forgotten.

— Oh, downcast geniuses who died there
In a barbarous circle that lacked sentiment —
By which you're a celebrity in the Orient,
Oh, sad country full of humour . . .

High School *Liceu*

High School — cemetery
Of all my youthful days —
Pedantic class teachers
And hard exams, always . . .
You still give me shudders
High School — cemetery
Of all my youthful days!

High School — cemetery
With long, long corridors —
Today I am no longer me
And my head feels sore . . .
I want nothing further —
High School — cemetery
With long, long corridors . . .

High School — cemetery
Of all my youthful days —
Into the world you sent me
In a whirlwind's craze,
Already life weary . . .
High School — cemetery
Of all my youthful days!

Prose *Proză*

Love, like a Satyr, hideous,
The decadent child —
Turned blue, beguiled,
Died yesterday, delirious.

Here, prosaic little creatures,
Have died upon their journey
Choked by jingling money,
In a world of shady shopkeepers.

Crises *Crize*

Sadly, behind a tree, on the field
The pale moon stays, in loneliness —
The wind is rattling the tree —
And I sense shivers of madness.

A muttering shadow advances . . .
It's human . . . that's all that's needed
And one will strangle the other, comrades:
He — who's hungry, I — who's satiated.

But you see . . . now it's me he's avoided . . .
The poor one was more afraid — you see . . .
Against the pale moon, in loneliness,
The wind is rattling the tree . . .

Prose *Proză*

It rains . . .
On a miserable town
Of mud and corn cobs,
On a town — Yiddified
That's full of shady shops
— And here my love stays . . .

And the alley is full
Of hay and corn cobs
And passing carters
With sacks of flour
And it rains even harder
On pubs even dirtier,
On a town — pauperized —
— And here my love stays . . .

It rains
On a town — Yiddified

Bountiful *Belşug*

Colours and smoke of autumn, a poet's misery
Water is cold, leaves are raining —
Speak slowly, step slowly.
As everything falls with a new sorrowing.

The wine, the honey, and all the grain
They gathered, in a hurry, who could today . . .
Cough and weeping create the dream,
Go somewhere else, leaf of clay . . .

And a small bird hints of winter
In the cold silence of a frosted garden —
I sneezed on a clean thoroughfare,
For not all the leaves have fallen.

There was a time . . . there'll be a time . . .
The horizon never says so, but man does —
The present deeply closes the tome . . .
Only now is as it never was . . .

I go to the same place, in the big building,
It is the hour for seclusion —
A nervousness . . . a numbing . . .
It's autumn . . . they give me the question . . .

Ego *Ego*

Even more silent and lonely
In my world that's empty —
And crushing me even more,
A hard misanthropy.

From all I've written, darling,
You must feel it too —
That lack of care I show
To people, and to you.

The Shoes *Pantofii*

Golden shoes, on show in the window,
On the night of the ball, you'll stay under frills,
And amid the waltz's lazy ripples
You'll laugh in ballrooms — a light in full flow.

On a sad catafalque, the sad queen won't know,
You'll still be on the icy, holy foot,
And as the times pass you'll burn in the vault,
Golden shoes, on show in the window . . .

A Storm *Furtună*

Through the forests of Bacău
Howls the wind
And clouds the world
A sky like the land —
And forest after forest
Is full of agitation,
And autumn's requiem
Is sung to them out loud . . .

And they seem to call me,
From hanging branches,
Moaning Absaloms
With plaits tangling . . .
From fear clutching me
Eyes are wandering,
And with all the noise, my brain
Understands nothing . . .

And I would like to die
As King Romulus did,
Forgotten, legendary . . .
Caught up in a storm,
Lost, to fade away
Through the forests of Bacău . . .

Twilight *Amurg*

At evening, on windows, a cloud of violet and of copper,
On the road, at the same hour, an iron chain drags itself,
And coincidences settle on a scale much sadder —
Today I'm afraid again . . . yet hope, have belief . . .

A day without a season or a military mind,
And in the vicinity one hears small sounds of dinner,
But things are harder now to find —
And many have left, and night settles lower.

With everyone saying how good were their deeds
Or that a genius will be born to us —
Again, tactfully taciturn, the process proceeds . . .
A supreme being, among us, knows us.

Hymn *Imn*

I

Thin branches with white flowers . . .
Lift me up
Raise me out of errors,
Ideals now lost to us . . .
With pink flowers, thin branches . . .
           Jesus!

Flowers on horizons, in the grass — flowers . . .
Lift me up
I've lived thousands of eras . . .
It is enough that you have left us . . .
Flowers on horizons, in the grass — flowers . . .
           Jesus!

II

To sleep . . .
To sleep and from there to die
Though everywhere there is a resurrection . . .
Look, they are empty,
Those sacred groves —
The poet has gone.

And if you are still looking,
Stepping on the secret spring,
You'll not see me —
The poet has gone . . .
To sleep . . .
To sleep, and from there to die
Though everywhere there is a resurrection . . .

Winter Dialogue *Dialog de iarnă*

The window is a poem of lead and sparks,
Snowed up the town's oblivion.
Since midnight the hours have passed later . . .
We cannot find ourselves in life's confusion . . .
Oh, come at least now, by an unknown power:
— Shall I come?
— Oh! I'm afraid . . .
— See!
— Come!
— I came;
— Where?
— To your side;
— I weep . . .
— I weep . . .
— Be quiet . . .
— Come . . .
— Come;
— To the infinite . . .
— To the infinite;
— Sing . . .
— Dream;
— Yes . . .
— No.
— No . . .
— Minus;
— Minus . . .
— Plus;
— Plus . . .
— Harmony.
— Harmony . . .
— When?
— When . . .
— Maybe;

— Maybe . . .
— Ah!
The window is a poem of lead and sparks . . .
A day invades the room with a frosty winter . . .
The sirens for the workers vibrate, doleful;
The city is an iceberg of smoke, of bell clangs,
And of thrill . . .
— Where . . . Where?!

Nocturne *Nocturnă*

In the citadel's night, I run that way, this,
In the tower, midnight is rarely struck;
It's the hour when bitter thoughts strike,
Silence . . . it's the hour of cowardice . . .

You lose yourself in empty loneliness,
Oh, soul, always running from them all;
It's the hour when Peter gives a bitter howl —
Listen . . . it is the hour of cowardice . . .

Somewhere Else *Aiurea*

Cursed should be the autumn,
And the leaf that drops on us —
Cursed should be the small town
Sullen, and with rain that's endless . . .

Citadel — a home for wasting away —
Snowdrifts from the Pole for bedding . . .
Citadel, the poet will die today
In your arms, coughing . . .

Psalm   *Psalm*

With death-like face, my love, you seem
A virgin forgotten in a castle,
On a balcony crying alone
With the same lifeless tone,
With a reticent soul —
You are there in my dream.

With death-like face, my love, you seem
A bride on a throne,
With the same lifeless tone
You are there in my dream.

With death-like face, my love, you seem
With just a flash of genius,
Yet the tone forever lifeless,
A Madonna in nakedness
Dusted by lilies —
You are there in my dream . . .

Contrast *Contrast*

Woman, — mask of colours,
Coquette full of nicety —
You, who yells at late night debauchery
You're not likely to thrill the dreamers . . .

Oh, there are pale-cheeked virgins still
White models with a fine form —
And they sleep alone, white and calm
In white cots of crystal . . .

A Ballad   *Baladă*

A night of sea-blue from times of the Voivodes . . .
The Voievode had left for one of the cursed battles;
And I was guarding the Princess locked in the fortress —
A night of sea-blue, of triumphal epochs . . .

The soldiers slept deeply in the diaphanous night,
When I came out hurriedly from my silken tent —
I saw on the horizon a half-moon nearly set,
And dazed, thought it — the Ottoman crescent.

With bewildered troops, I set off, at once, with horses,
But the night breeze led us straight back to the fortress
And relating my dream to the terrified princess,
I pointed with my sword to the picture in the distance.

In white, the blonde princess, in the ideal night,
On high, from a window, as in a dream took flight,
Bathed in sea-blue light, she laughed in the serene night . . .
Oh, how long the Princess laughed that sea-blue night . . .

Vobiscum   *Vobiscum*

In this world's circle banal and greedy . . .
A cry greatly convulses me deep down;
And this way (of being) will be till doom,
And nothing in this world startles me.

But alas, those defeated and lost for ever . . .
Either in garrets or tavern yards;
And the mad one, the silent, the wanderer,
Gesticulating on boulevards . . .

Twilight   *Amurg*

Colourful bourgeois ladies passing
In carriages of crystal —
It is an eternal promenade,
A millionaire's bedlam . . .

On public terraces
Weeping violins, sentimental . . .
There is perfume, candies,
A brothel of sensualism . . .

. . . But the proletarian philosopher
Writes in the book of the time:
Strikes, blood, madness,
Hunger,
Weeping — universal . . .
While twilight pours flames
Upon a finale already foretold
In a billionaire's mansion . . .

Piano *Piano*

And again all are sad,
Today as yesterday —
Floods of pain stay.

And the dream settles
Into black doom . . .

And better times
Don't come, never come,
No comfort, not a ray . . .

And again all are sad,
Today as yesterday.

Mystery   *Mister*

The pianos weep in town
At a time when autumn's so empty . . .
And the poplars also weep in town,
And everything is in its last agony.

The houses seem sad castles . . .
All love has died here
And, perhaps, weeping on pianos
Virgins with unplaited hair . . .

I walk alone . . . and lately I'm afraid . . .
And from where I am, cannot guess —
Ah, the poplars annihilate the town . . .
The pianos weep in emptiness . . .

Vae Soli *Vae soli*

I'll wait for you somehow, any day or any night
To see if there is anything I can do about it.
I'll pass again close to water, and in ripples see myself
                                                      appearing
I'll rest close to some ruins, again an owl will be weeping;
In the end there'll be no time . . . I'll be the worker that's
                                                      forgotten,
And for me too the world will be an accidental
                                            phenomenon . . .
As to love, I'll find it in a book — eventually,
Maybe a mirror will wound some compassionate bee —
I'll feel useless weeping at dawn, face to the sun,
I'll think of all the grief of poets long gone . . .
Winter will freeze me and over the house a raven will pass,
The town under snow at night will sing out from pianolas,
Or naked autumn will dance with plaits of wine and wheat
So that newcomers will no longer be able to compete . . .

At the Altar *În altar*

There is no sense in a cathedral
Today, in this century of niceties –
Now they come only in a frenzy,
Lovers with broken hearts.

. . . And frenzied, as the choir goes by
Thoughts grow more bitter —
They want a night of orgy
On the cloth of the altar . . .

The Final Poem *Poemă finală*

I must drink to forget what's known to no one,
Hidden in the deep cellar, but not speaking out,
Alone, to smoke there, unknown to anyone,
Otherwise, on earth it's difficult . . .

Let life and death howl on the streets,
Let poets weep their futile poetry . . .
I understand . . .
But the dreadful hunger's no joke, no dream —
Lead and storm, wasteland
Finis . . .
Contemporary history . . .
The time has come . . . all my nerves feel desire . . .
Oh, come at once, you grand future.

I must leave, to forget what's known by no one,
Saddened by bourgeois crimes never discussed,
Alone to get lost in the world, unknown to anyone,
Otherwise, on earth it's difficult . . .

Violated Sepulcres *Sepulcre violate*

Tramping in a pale twilight,
I entered the gates of the graveyard —
There the pallbearers joked with the dead,
And I laughed the laugh of a down-and-out.

Oh, the laughter of down-and-outs . . .
And what I saw was unusual
For in a tree I found a skull,
On a cross some blonde plaits.

Epitaph   *Epitaf*

'Here am I
Solitary
Who laughed bitterly
Always ready to cry.

As to my aspect
It was better to die,
Since to all I
Appeared suspect.'

Enough *Destul*

When I'm less troubled, I will write a verse
In which you'll see how I've been neglected —
Trying to decipher what I'd put there first,
Truly, I hardly knew what I wanted . . .

Weeping, I told myself never to weep again —
I was having . . .
Who knows, not I, what I was thinking
That other time, in my leafy den!

I'll write a verse, when I'm more settled . . .

On the Hill *Pe deal*

That's the answer
Why with an evil smile
I look at this night . . .
From steeps and dips
Of past times:
Ileana* . . .
Tales of yesteryear . . .
That's the answer
Why once again
With an evil smile
I look at
The benighted summits . . .

* *Ileana Cosânzeana was known as Helen the Goldbraided*

At the End   *Din urmă*

Poetry, poetry . . .
Yellow, lead, violet . . .
And the empty street . . .
Or waiting up late,
And frozen parks . . .
Poet, and unsociable . . .
Yellow, lead, violet . . .
The empty room . . .
And late nights . . .
Mourning perfume
And venerable . . .
For eternity . . .

In Fact Comedies
Comedii în fond 1936

Regret (*Regret*) / 169
Perhaps Tomorrow (*Ca mâine*) / 170
When Alone (*Când singur*) / 171
From The Past (*Din vremuri*) / 172
From a Lyre (*Din liră*) / 173
Towards Spring (*Spre primăvară*) / 174
About Winter (*De iarnă* 'Un hoit,
    un corb, un câmp și eu . . .') / 175
Gaudeamus (*Gaudeamus*) / 176
Verses (*Versuri* 'Un cântec trist din liră . . .') / 177
Serenade (*Serenadă* 'Poetizează luna . . .') / 178
Silence (*Tăcere*) / 179
From The Past (*Din vremuri*) / 180
The Day of Wrath (*Dies Irae*) / 181
Echo of a Love Song (*Ecou de romanță*) / 182
At the Shore (*La țărm*) / 183
Courage (*Curaj*) / 184
Late Echo (*Ecou târziu*) / 185
Clouds Are Passing (*Trec nouri*) / 186
Pastel (*Pastel* 'Sărmanii plopi de lângă moară . . .') / 187
Renunciation (*Renunțare*) / 188
Sunset (*Apus*) / 189
Echo of a Love Song (*Ecou de romanță*
    'Eu nu te mai văd . . .') / 190
In Somno (*In somno*) / 191
Twilight (*Amurg* 'Tristeți pe vânt . . .') / 192

Evening (*Seară* 'Ce este cerul — ...') / 193
Let's Make Love (*Să ne iubim*) / 194
Memento (*Memento*) / 195
Sometimes (*Vreodată*) / 196
Days Pass (*Trec zile*) / 197
Elegy (*Elegie*) / 198
Verses (*Versuri* 'Acorduri, arpegii, armonii ...') / 199
End of Autumn (*Sfârșit de toamnă*) / 200
Nihil (*Nihil*) / 201
Veritas (*Veritas*) / 202
Long Ago (*Demult*) / 203
A Legend (*Legendă*) / 204
A Song (*Un cântec*) / 205
And All (*Și toate*) / 206
Summer Night (*Noapte de vară*) / 207
Pastel (*Pastel* 'Tăcute locuri ...') / 208
In Happiness (*În fericire*) / 209
Controversy (*Controversă*) / 210
A Ballad (*Baladă* 'Clopot de alarma la mănăstire ...') / 211
Midday of Summer (*Miazăzi de vară*) / 212
Requiem (*Requiem*) / 213

Regret *Regret*

For a long, long time I've known two poplars
That I see even now as I pass —
I like so much to watch them,
But they fill me with sadness . . .

They seem to be saying 'I don't know' . . .
That maybe tomorrow I shall die —
Then they'll never be watched again
By any passer by . . .

Perhaps Tomorrow *Ca mâine*

With the star that's cut loose,
Now in chaos soon to be lost —
A heart maybe snuffed out
Towards eternal rest.

Perhaps tomorrow it'll be ours that go
Into austere eternity —
And who is going to worry?
Alas, no one . . . but you never know!

When Alone *Când singur*

When I see myself alone again
My name soon to be recalled,
With so many hopes . . .
I say to myself: It's late —
Oh, thoughts,
            In the world!

When inspired by vivid memories
You still believe in wry words
Or in the mysteries of drinking . . .
I say to myself: It's late —
Oh, thoughts,
            In the world!

And when you are next to nothing,
When you seek to be lauded,
Far too late . . .
I say to myself: It's late —
Oh, thoughts,
            In the world!

From The Past *Din vremuri*

For a moment let me consider . . .
How winter sets about its terror —
Miseries sing sadly much closer,
Windows glitter from the hoar.

Wintery nights' storms burst . . .
But who looks for grandeur
That lures us from the past?
Windows glitter from the hoar.

From a Lyre   *Din liră*

If by now it's late,
And my eyes are wet no longer —
I've come to realise . . .
You've gone, forever!

And if that was all . . .
And in cold shadow I hover —
I've come to realise . . .
You've gone, forever!

Towards Spring *Spre primăvară*

From the eaves it drips . . .
With a rumour of great eras —
I'll smile just for a bit —
Rise up, proletarian workers!

From horizons that are widening
They leave these unknown glaciers —
Under skies with songs and flowers —
Rise up, proletarian workers!

About Winter *De iarnă*

A corpse, a raven, a field and me,
Winter . . . and snow begins to fly —
Everywhere the snow reaches the sky . . .
No one, just snow, snowing constantly.

— Oh, raven!
What use is a blind soul to man . . .
That comes alone to the wasteland —
Where years blow by like sand.
Oh, raven!
What use is a blind soul to man . . .
— You're right!

— Oh, raven!
What use is a blind soul to man . . .
— Delays, enclosed tomb —
Do we live, or is it all a dream —
Oh, raven!
What use is a blind soul to man . . .
— You're right!

It's late, and it snows, night is falling,
I'm all on my own . . .
No one's about on the streets of the town —
I'm back home, peace, nothing!

Gaudeamus   *Gaudeamus*

Thwarted flutes play
On such pagan days —
Aspirations blown to the wind,
Nothing now remains . . .

In wind and forgetting, all stay
Mastered by difficult days —
Of anybody, anything of their lives,
Nothing now remains . . .

Verses   *Versuri*

From my life, I'd still like
To throw you a sad song
From my lyre into the darkness
Of deep non-understanding.

Is it really an illusion . . .
Is everything collapsing?
Worshipping whispers
And my deep suffering —
If at any time they were —
And future visions —
Look, I throw them to you . . .
— It's my lyre's sad song.

Serenade *Serenadă*

The moon poetizes
Your beloved lattice —
Through the hidden shadows
I wait for you as I did before —
With my weeping on the chords,
At our secret place —
And which perhaps once
In this world gave you pleasure.

The moon poetizes
The garden full of perfumes —
The prosaic hoards
Are noisy no more . . .
Through the hidden shadows,
A stranger as always —
With my weeping on the chords,
I wait for you as I did before.

Silence *Tăcere*

What more is there ... books for the night —
I still read and feel that I am here —
Who else has the lamp burning
At such a late hour?

On the table a clock is ticking ...
Of all that exists, shouldn't I be aware?
The night ...
Who else has the lamp burning
At such a late hour?

From The Past   *Din vremuri*

It's cold, winter . . .
I want to think of my wasted years —
I no longer wait for anyone,
No hope either.
No one is free any more . . .
I want to think of my wasted years —
Close up everything,
Close the door — it's cold, winter.

The Day of Wrath   *Dies Irae*

How strange I feel in my own country
I've no longing left in me —
An evil and darkened thought
Silences all impartiality.

It will be too late on that day . . .
Many ravages on my way
The silence of the times, dreadful hunger!
Or songs that always weep:
— Hurry, wait no longer!

Echo of a Love Song   *Ecou de romanță*

It's gone — that clear blue,
And spring has run down–
I've waited in a long sigh for you,
              You didn't come!

And withered are the fields,
And summer with its nights, has gone —
I've waited for you among the limes,
              You didn't come!

Later on, autumn left too,
All the greenery has wandered, has run —
Weeping on streets I called to you,
              You didn't come!

And, tomorrow, in winter's sad waste,
You'll never hear from me again —
Don't ever come, it's far too late,
              Don't ever come!

At the Shore   *La țărm*

Oh, bitter thought . . .
Loneliness.
Wandering springtime evenings,
Perfumes fled on the wind —
And flutes from rocks of the sea . . .
— Once, once upon a time . . .
And waves murmuring on the shore,
Disquieting expectations,
Loneliness,
And flutes
From rocks of the sea . . .

Courage   *Curaj*

Although with the winter that's gone
It could seem that I'd died there —
Torrents poured from heavy snows . . .
Song after song made me stir.

Garrulous voices told me then
About a life no matter how gruelling . . .
And the sun on high and a sky opened
Full of the joys of spring.

Late Echo *Ecou târziu*

Sound of cembaloes, late into the night . . .
Like a vulgar show —
Women yelling, shamming frenzy
Through the reek of tobacco.

There were newspapers, events
Of critical times, or regrets, —
Suspicious shadows of cabarets . . .
There were newspapers, events.

Sound of cembaloes, late in the night . . .
Like a vulgar show —
Women yelling, shamming frenzy
Through the reek of tobacco.

Clouds Are Passing *Trec nouri*

Today I'm writing nothing more.
One cigarette, and one glass —
And the noons of each day fly
Like a symptom quick to pass.

What is important to remember,
Right here, or on the grass –
The noons of each day fly
Like a symptom quick to pass.

Pastel *Pastel*

Poor poplars at the side of the mill
How they stand alone in loneliness —
And over them it still snows . . .
Poor poplars at the side of the mill!

As dark thoughts fall upon me,
Thinking I'll die one of these nights . . .
So ravens fall upon their heights —
As dark thoughts fall on me.

Renunciation   *Renunțare*

In the dead garden
Last night I jumped over a wall, still dead,
My slow step was pulled up on the spot —
Fully aware of destiny, blind to sorrow
In the dead garden
        Someone arrived — dead . . .

Looking at the garden, still dead
The white moon, still dead –
Onto the stone bench
My body fell like lead.

From outside one could hear
Proletarian life there —
Only my shadow was behind the wall, still dead,
Now forever more, it weeps through the night . . .
In the garden, still dead
        Someone arrived — dead.

Sunset *Apus*

Since my closed soul
Wants nothing more —
Leaves fall at twilight,
My Dear!

Sinister night
And bitter star —
Soon it will snow,
My dear!

Echo of a Love Song   *Ecou de romanță*

I don't see you any more...

In vain there is sun, and an ideal sky —
Always closer comes life's reality...
Therefore, my darling, I don't see you any more!

I don't see you any more...

And the goblet is empty, and hallowed the wine —
Late serenades with those secret lines
Are gone... and closer comes life's reality...

My darling, I don't see you any more!

In Somno *In somno*

Harsh rows,
Ugly words,
Leave far into the night
Where you now belong,

— Any illusions
Where have they gone?

Who would know
When I am alone —
Who would listen
To my pain . . .

— I didn't hear
There is silence!

Harsh rows,
Ugly words,
Leave far into the night
Where you now belong.

Twilight   *Amurg*

Sadness on the wind, sadness of the dead
Scatter silently on the street —
Late feasts with new wine,
Dreams for a poor poet . . .

Those times so happily spent
Will me, lonely, to stay, now —
Towards autumn, sweet sighs
From Eminescu, Heine and Lenau . . .

Evening *Seară*

What sky is it — or has the day gone . . .
In chirruping twilight I'm here for you, waiting —
Now that's all that's left for me . . .
To complete happiness, that's where I'm going!

And you feel they're talking about you
Nearby, far away — is my brain still working?
What day is it — either the day has gone . . .
Or I'll always stay listening to the twilight chirruping.

Let's Make Love   *Să ne iubim*

Alas, there will come a time
When we'll fall asleep the two of us,
And estranged in cemeteries
It'll be autumn that weeps for us.

What matter then — if under the sun
Within the chaos of boundlessness —
You lose your virginity
In the pink secret of voluptuousness?

Memento   *Memento*

And while the snowstorm wanders . . .
The hours of the clock have rasped
The sufferings of dead souls —
Though . . . these are things of the past!

And while the snowstorm wanders . . .
Once again, loves that were lost
Awaken lonely poets —
Though . . . these are things of the past!

And while the snowstorm wanders . . .
As on an unknown coast . . .
Once more I think that you are lovely —
Though . . . these are things of the past!

Sometimes *Vreodată*

. . . And I'll take from the sky
What I no longer
Find among the stars,
Since I began to wander.

I prefer to think like this
When I yearn eagerly —
Or the sky is cold
To infinity . . .

Days Pass *Trec zile*

Days flow towards cemeteries
Sadly one by one,
And unbraiding life's threads
Are then forever gone.

And there, gently, and very low
They gather around sighing —
Yearning for their sister, 'tomorrow',
Yearning for my being.

Elegy *Elegie*

When I'm again crazy and unwell,
In sanatoriums, or hospitals,
I'll stay watching
The waltz of life
And other things, — like an adieu . . .

In sanatoriums, or hospitals,
Anyway, against my will —
Perhaps I'll be alone.
Then, silence . . .
As in autumn, a twilight of troubles . . .

Verses *Versuri*

Chords, arpeggios, harmonies . . .
They made me do what they wanted,
— To linger with my wasted years,
— To weep late into the early hours,
In the sad hours, unfathomed.
Chords, arpeggios, harmonies.

End of Autumn   *Sfârșit de toamnă*

In the grove with heaps of rusted leaves
There was a quiet cold . . .
A pink and violet medley
Has settled over palaces —

Deserted was the shrubbery . . .
None knew how the silence took hold —
Or why no one breathes . . .
A small bird warbles:
           — Ready?

Nihil *Nihil*

What love to sigh
    To long
    To throng
With those who die.

And what a bound
    To judder,
    Forever
Into the ground.

And how inane
    Living
    Thinking
If you've never been.

And what a word . . .
    Mystery,
    Heavenly,
And on earth.

Veritas *Veritas*

Oh Lord! The need for wine and more . . .
And to reach my zenith of poetry at last —
Anyway what else would I be sighing for:
. . . Above all, perhaps its magic is fast.

As in a solemn silence of a dome,
Life seems to pass without any sense . . .
And those expectations in the life of man —
                . . . Sana mens!

Long Ago   *Demult*

Going along your streets
Now unknown to anybody —
The rustling of night incites:
      — Philosophy!

Slowly, a watchman pipes
Such tardy poetry ...
The emptiness of night incites:
      — Philosophy!

A Legend *Legendă*

When anything is for sale,
When anything can be sold –
There rises from an ancient harp
A song from days of old.

From goblets, wine for forgetting,
Let a scarf be for virtue upheld —
There rises from an ancient harp
A song from days of old.

A Song   *Un cântec*

How sad in this world
Is a song,
A song I often hear

— To work . . .

In the dawn hours of spring
In the late nights of winter
Who could possibly start,
A song,
Without an end,
That we've forgotten over the years,
Chaotic
And without sense . . .
Who could possibly start
A song for living
At the deserted door
Of my late years . . .

How sad in this world
Without an end,
Is a song that I often hear:

— To work!

And All *Și toate*

And they all return their own way,
And proud spring will be here,
With gentle sun, with blue nights,
Enchanting and clear.

But without it, what keepsake
Wills me on towards sad meditation?
Buds have burst on the bough — in vain,
Inside my heart there's autumn!

Summer Night *Noapte de vară*

The night slowly settles, quietly —
Poetry or destiny —
The moon climbs sleepily,
        Come, come to me!

It is quiet, and cool,
The forest is full of fantasy —
Under the lindens still in bloom, —
        Poetry, or destiny.

In sweet scents unfurled,
Poetry or destiny —
Wherever you are in the world —
        Come, come to me!

The angels above us in flight
Are singing of all that's holy —
Ah, what a clear blue night —
        Poetry, or destiny.

Pastel *Pastel*

Silent places . . . the breeze
On the river bridge . . . it's melting —
Ravens . . .
Meaning what ? . . . Living.

As in the past, nobody . . .
In violet fog boughs swaying —
The breeze on the river bridge . . .
Bourgeois horizons . . . Living.

In Happiness *În fericire*

There are moments when I have it all . . .
Silent, sweet psychoses —
Lovely tales like dreams of roses . . .
There are times when I have it all . . .

See, there are moments when I have it all . . .
Life is spent with words in a row —
A song from the past . . . long ago . . .
There are times when I have it all . . .

Controversy *Controversă*

It wasn't my time for story-telling,
But I listened to what was said —
How hard to understand when gazing
On the face of the dead.

'That young man was far too lonely!
Yet he was loved everywhere . . .
— Well then, if he wasn't lonely,
Maybe the others weren't either.

And he once had a young lady —
And into the world they set out —
You felt you would start to cry
Between the questions they asked.

But see, from all this, came nothing —
An angel's birth came about . . .
— Thus, all these were just nothing.
And at once all fell silent!

Return embodied in others or alone
Then you'll understand the stories —
That young man, so very alone
Is now among old timers.'

It wasn't my time for story-telling,
But I listened to what was said,
How hard to understand when gazing
On the face of the dead.

A Ballad *Baladă*

In the monastery, alarm bell, commotion . . .
'The fall of the Devils' — midnight —
The ripe fruit of the times quite
Locks the past — it's liberation.

Among monks, what buzzings, whispers,
Fleeing torches return in confusion.
And surely, with dawn's horizon
We'll still have in mind these vespers!

. . . And the bell chimes, chimes . . .
'Satan is defeated' — no compassion —
The heart is awake expecting new times.

Are they bad dreams? A chimera of sight? —
— On the sky, in the background, signs —
A conscience from a very long night.

Midday of Summer   *Miazăzi de vară*

A simple bourgeois Sunday ...
Song of a broken organ,
What old ballad still weeps
On the embankment — all of a sudden?

An echo both secular and late ...
And the scorching day, a ruin —
— A sombre German ballad
On the streets, but the citadel is Latin.

Requiem *Requiem*

I was about to wait in the park
Noticing that here loneliness had stopped me . . .
But always the same forgettings!
But, ad infinitum, always the same poetry!

The philosophy of life told me:
There is somewhere, further than it looks . . .
So on and so on . . . leave it!
One dreams, as in books!

Bourgeois Verses
Stanțe Burgheze, 1946

Sic Transit . . . (*Sic transit . . .*) / 217
Stimulation (*Antrenare*) / 218
Ideas (*Idei*) / 219
The First May Day (*Arminden*) / 221
A Study (*Studiu*) / 222
Autumn in the Town (*Toamnă în târg*) / 223
Sine Die (*Sine die*) / 224
A Stanza to Wine (*Stanță la vin*) / 225
Urban Aesthetics (*Estetic urban*) / 226
Meridian (*Meridian*) / 227
Nihil Novi (*Nihil novi*) / 228
The Visit (*Visita*) / 229
Warm Afternoon (*După-amiază caldă*) / 230
Excelsior (*Excelsior*) / 231
Stop Press (*De ultima oră*) / 232
Perpetuum Mobile (*Perpetuum mobile*) / 233
Nocturnal Hibernation (*Hibernal noptat*) / 234
Modern (*Modernă*) / 235
Gloss (*Glossă*) / 236
About Art (*De artă*) / 237
Bohemian (*Boemă*) / 238

Sic Transit . . .   *Sic transit . . .*

I

There, where there is nobody,
Nor shadows,
Where a multitude
Of years pass,
And the noise of the street,
And the silence of night . . .
Where everything is known . . .
There, travellers write,
That only squalls of fire
Are seen
Lugubrious, metallic,
From minute to minute.
There, where there is nobody,
And there is no longer
The need for words.

II

And look, suddenly it is evening
All day nothing has happened.
The same
As so often before.
Stories . . .
About work,
Laziness,
The banquet in the shadows,
Or a time for happiness.
And look, suddenly it is evening,
All day nothing has happened.

Stimulation   *Antrenare*

At the meeting place
I waited.
For a while
The hours pass
Distressingly.
This is what I thought.
About you,
I said to myself
That you take me
Into a world
That lasts long,
As in a room with books,
Where as much as one speaks
Has also been written.
And in the language
I know,
There are many topics
On the science of versification.
So, describe it,
While distressingly
The hours pass.

Ideas *Idei*

I

Song over the citadel,
Growing old?
I said to Eternity:
With this beautiful music
There are defects
In my blood.
Angels above the citadel,
Excited
About something new?
Telegraph,
A telephone from spheres . . .
There are defects
In my blood.

II

Long smouldered visions
If I've not somehow
Lost my Shadow
Between the normal
And temptations.
Some wine,
No matter if a comforter,
Let it exclude this fate:
A contract
With the evil Dealer.

III

When free hours
Ring out
From the old accordion
About the bravados of days . . .

Relative,
Pardon.

When free hours
Ring out
Forgetting and abandon
On world's barricades . . .
Relative
Pardon.

The First May Day *Arminden*

Profile of a giant burg
And a rare atmosphere,
Bitter perfume of lilac
And sounds of a guitar.

Pleasures
Of a day of feasting and flowers,
Merry old customs . . .
Towards fields
And groves
Goes the heroic class of workers.

And next day,
Post festum —
Furtive signs of a cross
On streets
And in tramways,
For the necessary productivity
Of monotonous Labour.

A Study *Studiu*

Near violin strings
I listened
To the sad sound
To forget olden times,
Or my forgotten town.

But the violins' whispering
Showed me
More charged,
Streets with traces of loving . . .
And nor has the town changed.

Autumn in the Town *Toamnă în târg*

See, the fruit has been harvested,
The soul, used to sadness . . .
The winter birds flee
Towards decayed gardens.
Lasting love
Has become simply poetical.
This is no reason for one to cry.
Do you remember?
Dreams came to the country
From the Orient.
The seller was passing
With a basket of books.
Do you remember?
Short echoes,
And the hoar-frosted town.
Monotonous,
Gun shots of the hunters.

Sine Die *Sine die*

You should not
Speak your thoughts
If you regret
What your pen once wrote.

Let your mind linger in Non-being
Buzzings through the centuries,
There's nothing more to retain
Of the many things once murmured.

There isn't and never was;
Day after day has rolled.
An unsure horizon,
And metaphysical threshold.

A Stanza to Wine   *Stanță la vin*

Friends, it is the hour
When wine
Made us suspects.
Cadences
Of a slow time-piece.
If there was ever a time
Better than now,
Or one could sleep
The whole of tomorrow . . .
How from an upper floor
One sees
Motor cars
And a dwarfed world.
How youths
Look
In damp pubs.
Friends,
Cadences
Of a slow time-piece . . .
A coat in good taste,
Let us leave
The unknown
Leviathan.

Urban Aesthetics   *Estetic urban*

The town at night . . .
Worksites at rest.
Sign boards written
With starry bulbs.
The town at night . . .
In a square
With the glint of iron,
Car horns harmoniously blown.
The outskirts
With Bacchanal desires,
And thoughts
Of operas once seen.
The town at night . . .
From the static of forgetting —
Enough beauty,
Enough distance.

Meridian *Meridian*

The summer season is finished
With its blue serenades . . .
With star-hidden reveries . . .
— The poem that has ended.

The winter season has loomed
When the windows are hit by a blizzard . . .
When far away is frozen hard . . .
— The poem that has arrived.

Nihil Novi *Nihil novi*

I

I send you
These words
From near the burning lamp.
Now I'm going to bed,
Not to sleep
But to listen
To ridiculous echoes.
— If only dawn would come...
It's money
My thoughts centre on.
I toast to some of them,
To others I'm misunderstood again...
Whatever relaxes the night,
— If only dawn would come...

II

And summer days
And a clear horizon...
After another ten years,
What else will be known —
Thought, always unsuccessful.
Hope stays,
But with it
There's never a bound.
The swallows burst
Into boundlessness.

The Visit *Visita*

This century made me
So cultured,
That I tend to look
Down on people.
I've learned so much
Just lately,
That we have reached
An important moment.
One could make
Many reforms.
I was thinking out aloud.
Nobody about.
And only today
Some visitors came.
— What's in it for you, what's in it for me . . .
Oh, it's been so long, how lovely.

Warm Afternoon   *După-amiază caldă*

Since God
Moved me to write
These lines.
I was thinking,
Just to look at them.
To publish them,
Then perhaps,
From the shadow of a terrace,
One silent,
Sunny afternoon,
A bird will pass,
Far off,
As through a park . . .
You'll think back
To the splendid tale.

Excelsior *Excelsior*

Today superb,
Tomorrow sombre.
This is
Because I write well.
And, perhaps,
A store
Of dreams,
But a soul much braver . . .
Silences
Of the future.
But a soul much braver . . .
Beyond cancans,
Or teasing . . .
Oh, in the country,
With bourgeois souvenirs,
In a mansion . . .
A symphony
From the street
Changed me, musically . . .

Stop Press *De ultima oră*

War
Movement of nations.
Trade has ceased.
Bread,
Cornflour,
In alphabetical order.
Progress in science,
Signals,
Exploits,
Home,
Hut,
Shelter . . .
Red nights
Earthquake . . .
The world reignites.

Perpetuum Mobile *Perpetuum mobile*

I've not won
A single thought
I could write with.
Composer of words . . .
In colours,
Reveries,
Harmonies,
So as to pass over
The heavy silence.
Composer of words . . .
The world is changing.
Equality,
Tumultuous ideas,
Organization
Of the foreseen future.
There are degrees,
There are
Positions of responsibility . . .

Nocturnal Hibernation *Hibernal noptat*

I

When I pass
Through nights silently
And my mind
Imagines you
In mute agony . . .
Oh, dream, oh, ideal soul,
Love,
That would like to begin
Making you tremble with delight . . .
Oh, dream, oh, ideal soul,
Shouldn't they learn,
Those lovers from the past.

II

What shadow stays at your window
Like that of vanquished loves?
A past poet, and the emptiness
On snowy lanes.
A wintry weeping, settled,
In the hard, late hour,
With the cursed blizzard —
Running, who knows where . . .

Modern *Modernă*

I

A soprano
On the 'radio'
Folklore,
Aperitifs
Of brandy
And olives.
Classic lore,
In a castle
Far away
In the 18th century.
Teas,
Wafers
And candy.

II

And lo! Peace
And lo!
And again, lo!
A spellbound town.
Aeroplane.
A train,
A steamer.
A monster
Will be killed
By a hero.
There blasts
A loud speaker . . .
Mysteries
At the cinema.

Gloss *Glossă*

Look scholarly
With a heart drunk
From love
Static is nature.
Love is reborn
With the fire of summer,
With diamonds
Of winter.
Metempsychosis,
Metamorphosis,
And many more.
Good bye,
Or adieu.
Look scholarly.
If there's no one
One can talk to,
One writes.

About Art   *De artă*

The coffee party
With cursed dreamers.
Years have passed,
Symbolism,
The current, decadent.
Brochures,
Rare jewels.
Paradoxes,
The bizarre
Evenings,
Nights,
Gushes of perfumes
And nuances.
The town, dominant.

Bohemian *Boemă*

The snow was settling —
It was snowing.
I was wishing,
(And have done for many years)
To meet you
At the end of the street
That leads to the field.
It seemed to me
That you were lovelier
In winter.
Only the ravens told me
You stayed home
With some gentleman.
I returned to the town.
The snow was sparkling
Electrically
At your window.
A night was passing.
I was reading
As on nights in winter.

Stanzas and Verses
Stanțe și versețe, 1949–1954

Obsessions (*Obsesii*) / 241
Reflections (*Reflecții*) / 242
Resignation (*Resemnare*) / 243
Although Nothing (*Deși nimic*) / 244
Doina (*Doină* 'Frunze se tărăsc . . .') / 245
Old Stanza (*Stanță veche*) / 246
Noises (*Zgomote*) / 247
A Town Night (*Noapte de oraș*) / 248
Real Stanza (*Stanță reală*) / 249
Doina (*Doină* 'Poezia tace . . .') / 250
Medium Stanza (*Stanță medie*) / 251
Stanza for Bacovia (*Stanță la Bacovia*) / 252
Archaism (*Arhaism*) / 253
Doina (*Doină* 'Dintre câte-am încercat . . .') / 254
Plain Style (*Stil simplu* 'Ca suflet . . .') / 255
In the Village (*În sat*) / 257
Plain Style (*Stil simplu* 'Duruieli de nouri . . .') / 258
From Explorations (*Din explorări* 'Că, și ei aleargă . . .') / 259
From The Train (*Din tren*) / 260
Vanitas (*Vanitas*) / 261
Plain Style (*Stil simplu* 'În sunete lirice . . .') / 262
Pastel (*Pastel* 'Prea ursuz și plumburiu . . .') / 263
A Stanza of War (*Stanță de război*) / 264
From the Informer (*Informativ*) / 265
Darkness in the Town (*Negură-n oraș*) / 266
From Explorations (*Din explorări* 'Știu și ei . . .') / 267
Pro Arte (*Pro arte*) / 268

Worldly Stanza (*Stanță de lume*) / 269
Spleen (*Spleen*) / 270
Count (*Compt*) / 271
About Winter (*De iarnă* 'Chiciură, polei,
    cad oameni pe stradă . . .') / 272
Newsreel (*Jurnal*) / 273
Study (*Studiu*) / 274
Peace (*Pace*) / 275
Mythology (*Mitologie*) / 276
Cogito (*Cogito*) / 277
Destiny (*Destin*) / 278
Incident at the Ball (*Incident la bal*) / 279
Evening (*Seară* 'Liniște . . . nu se mișcă nimic . . .') / 280
In Winter (*În iarnă*) / 281
Thoughts (*Gândiri*) / 282
Chemistry (*Chimie*) / 283
Legend (*Legendă* '— Ce bine-a scris . . .') / 284
Pastel (*Pastel* 'E frig la câmp . . .') / 285
Libation (*Libelă*) / 286
Twilights (*Amurguri*) / 287
Moment (*Moment*) / 288
On the Horizon (*În zare*) / 289
Late Verse (*Verset târziu*) / 290
Epode (*Epodă*) / 291
New Year's Eve (*Revelion*) / 292
At Edges (*În margini*) / 294
Restorations (*Restituiri*) / 295
Fiefs (*Feude*) / 296
Ideal Verse (*Verset ideal*) / 297
Prosaic Verse (*Verset prozaic*) / 298
Serenade (*Serenadă* 'Serenadă plângătoare . . .') / 299
Fantastic Verse (*Verset fantast*) / 300
Slavic Verse (*Verset slav*) / 301

Obsessions *Obsesii*

Thinking only
Of you,
I kept meeting
Aspects of you.
It even seemed
They were you . . .
Except that your soul
Should always stay
Different.
And thus
On my journey
Diverse psychologies
Banished me
To the heavy marching
Of the street.

Reflections   *Reflecții*

Today I thought —
Art —
Intending
To write
An interesting novel.
But the hour was hard . . .
In the end,
All was silence.
I was thinking
Of Art
A novel . . .
— People keep talking
About that hero.

Resignation *Resemnare*

As a poet,
I'd describe you.
Describe your splendid gestures —
Coming from my longing,
It would lose something,
When I read you
In verses.

As a painter,
I'd paint you —
You'd be my living icon;
Coming from my longing,
I'd forget something
When I looked you
In the face.

As a musician
I'd whisper to you
With a flute,
Or with strings–
Coming from my longing,
It would continue
To recall you forever.

Although Nothing   *Deși nimic*

How much I suffered
Loving
Your face,
In my school-boy room . . .
And, perhaps, you were thinking
Of me.
Although nothing . . .
Like the din
Of a piano
Like rain,
Or shrieking violins
Fit only for monkeys . . .
Although nothing . . .
— Then, the fanfare of living,
The office
And erudite speeches . . .

Doina *Doină*

Leaves crawling . . .
Chemistry on the wind
So many needs.
I imagine:
When strolling through the park,
Last summer we . . .
Shouting on the wind,
At a sleepy window,
New ideals . . .

Old Stanza   *Stanță veche*

I want to believe
I lived
In luxury . . .
What a feeling,
Sad from now onwards . . .
Words,
About work,
Wages
Or dramatic verses.
Wishful thinking —
Beloved times
That once were
Or will come again . . .
What a feeling . . .
Hatred . . .
Here, there,
Forgetting . . .

Noises   *Zgomote*

Without reason what fear
Has installed . . .
They are the joys
Of the subconscious
That fall at the window
Like an unexpected darkness,
They are the town's
Intimidations,
Enigmas of hazard
And years that have fled,
Senseless
And whispers of forgetting —
If it were so
What would happen . . .

A Town Night   *Noapte de oraș*

I

On the wet cobbles,
Clip clop of horseshoes,
Buses rumbling
And torch lights sliding
On windows lighting
Dark rooms.
With tardy tick-tock,
With weeping silences,
With the rainy night
That's outside . . .

II

It rains . . .
I know nothing . . .
For days, for years,
The same life,
Without finding
Out about any other life . . .
The same tardy tick-tack,
With weeping silences,
From no special time . . .
Like the rainy night
That's outside . . .

Real Stanza   *Stanță reală*

The sarcastic, senseless
Laugh
Of anxiety
From one day to the next . . .
In the short pause
For reconciliation
In a sad silence
Watching . . .
When we awaken
From the tomb!

Poetic secret . . .
Clumps of trees
And solitary hills —
The earth . . .
Goes off barking
In wasteland
And woods
With beasts
Also the wild sleep . . .
When we awaken
From the tomb!

Doina *Doină*

Poetry is silent
On quarrel days . . .
And many questions
About government . . .
The little bit of everything
Where has it ended?
When at the rung of man,
When animal . . .
Towards light,
Towards darkness . . .
As time is passing
It is not enough . . .
. . . And perhaps
Every thought
Has been said . . .

Medium Stanza *Stanță medie*

I don't know if
These stanzas
Are understood . . .
But they give me
Pleasure.
They speak
About a frail
Soul
In the rush
Of barbarians . . .
And when everything
And everyone
Become mute
Perhaps
Only then
Life will become
Better than ever.
But these stanzas
Are understood . . .
They are alive,
A frail
Soul
In the rush
Of barbarians . . .

Stanza for Bacovia   *Stanță la Bacovia*

To a poet

And voices
In echoing valleys . . .
Bacovia,
Country of delight
And a peaceful life.
One does not talk
About mine
And yours
Or fear
Of death.
Bacovia,
Country
Of invigorating
Song:
In front of you,
And then,
Everywhere . . .
Beasts too
Obeyed
The man.
Bacovia,
The country
When any thought
Is silent . . .

Archaism *Arhaism*

A star fled
From the firmament . . .
And drops of fire,
Incoherent,
Vanished
With it.

Why was I the only one
Who saw it,
And I ask myself:
Whose is it?
Whatever it was,
It was!
Not needed . . .
A world
Was well overdue . . .

Doina *Doină*

As much as I have tried
Not one wish have I realised . . .
Perhaps tomorrow
Or the next morrow,
It'll be sweet
That bread.

And as I sit here so upset,
Every single thing I've left . . .
Only you gave me support
And in the world
Again talked.

Plain Style *Stil simplu*

I

Like a soul
That's fallen,
An autumn sky,
Heavy,
Delays
The hopes
Of yesterday.
And leaves,
Years
Flying
Through the world,
In vain . . .
We expect nothing
With winter
Approaching —
Except
It will snow.

II

Thus,
A sadness
Entered
The town
With the rain,
This morning.
And crows
Cawing.
One can scarcely
Read
The paper.

One feels —
Like staying at home . . .
. . . Ah, it wasn't so
In our day . . .

In the Village   *În sat*

It snows in the village
Far away.
Here, and there,
Rising smoke —
Through the snow
*Bordeie sleep
As if no one
Is living.
Yet
They say
That some beast
From the forest
Sets the dogs
Barking . . .

* *A house built into the ground with a roof covered in grass.*

Plain Style *Stil simplu*

Thunder
From clouds,
Rain
And wind —
Fiery lightning,
Muddy days,
Thunderbolts
Strike home —
Moments of sadness,
Maybe flown away . . .
Muddy days,
How long will they
Remain . . .

From Explorations *Din explorări*

That they too
Run
The whole day,
Giving one thing
For another.
One produces,
One decides
Upon an interest
For
A certain time.
One eats —
A serenade,
And nothing is important.

From The Train *Din tren*

The carriage ran
Forwards.
The field of work,
The field of world
Were dragged
Behind.
The warm
And solar day
Revealed beautiful flowers.
At night,
A falling star
Searched around
And disappeared.
When the carriage
Halted
Between walls,
The field of work
And of world,
Beyond walls —
Seemed
Not to exist.

Vanitas *Vanitas*

I can no longer sing you
Love songs,
They are all silent
Around me,
The course of life,
Goes treacherously
Never finding
A new song . . .
My love for me was
A secret agent,
Finally unmasked
But I don't know when . . .
I can no longer sing you
Love songs,
And of course,
I've forgotten them . . .

Plain Style   *Stil simplu*

In lyrical strains
That are joyful
That have interesting
Intentions . . .
— Not one moment
Spent in vain —
Perhaps the day
Has passed.
Evening's near.
Dinner,
To bed . . .
To know nothing more . . .
— Except, a very special dream.

Pastel *Pastel*

Too sullen
And leaden
The sky came down
Over the slums.
Screaming pigs,
Ghostly roosters
Of hunger
Provoking
Winter
Death.
— The pencil,
The lead,
Would like
To render
A violet
Letter
From the slums.

A Stanza of War   *Stanță de război*

I

Time after time
Lying down,
I note
The world's rumour,
Of a new country.
Moderate capital —
— Honour to intellectuals —
— And to those who work.
But what will be their future,
— At the moment it is sublime . . .

II

Besieging
By starving,
Conflagration,
Waves of blood.
In such circumstances
To keep on going
Even as a poet . . .
And after triumphant marches,
In the rhythm of happy tunes,
Everything hums
As in a story.

From the Informer   *Informativ*

A manifesto,
A Fair
Of principles
Took refuge
In the citadel —
Work!
Party!
And rest again.
— We don't eat
Cheese,
But fruit.
We don't complicate
The manifesto,
We communicate
With partisans.

Darkness in the Town *Negură-n oraş*

Under the morose
November sky
Impressions
Of what is most sad
And most rainy.
Recalling
For much later
A clear one.
Under the morose
November sky,
At the gloomy window,
Like flippant leaves,
A soul weeps,
Settled down,
Dreaming an inspiration
— To shower sparks.

From Explorations *Din explorări*

I

... They also know
How to live
Something
Familiar,
Social,
Which they strictly follow.
The same language,
Expensive objects
Put in their place.
Individualism,
Altruism,
Communism,
— Time patina
Got them closer
To *Homo sum.*

II

Minutes of smouldering
And mumblings ...
Wordly images,
A misanthrope,
Singular male ...
Sarcastic chief
From a distance ...
— To pick yourself up, to laugh ...
*'And the last fight let us face ...'

---

* *First line of the refrain from the Communist Song 'Internationala'*

Pro Arte *Pro arte*

I

In ephemeral
Stanzas
Any pleasures
Have gone . . .
If you return
From chaos
One hears —
— There was,
— There was . . .
Then plant out,
A newer
And more positive
Sign.

II

I write
And perhaps,
I reveal
A moral crisis,
Without knowing it —
The reader
Would object.
I eat
To live.
I write
To get cleverer.
The contagion
Of my sad moral,
Esteemed reader,
Forget it —
Like other books.

Worldly Stanza *Stanță de lume*

So much sadness
My grief
Had spoken of . . .
Grandeur
Of old ruins
Or isolations —
In the town
Park . . .
With little money
And never
Richer —
Poor artist
Or drunkard,
Led hand in hand
By policemen,
As immoral
To the Informers'
Bureau . . .
I was in the park,
Of a medieval
And commercial
Town.

Spleen *Spleen*

Variation . . .
Architecture,
Destination,
Silence.
Music calms
A sad soul,
That became pretentious.
Variety . . .
Famous,
From a work of art . . .
Theories old and new . . .
Silence —
One laughs, and from the belly.

Count *Compt*

In a recess . . .
A thought
Through darkness —
Genial . . .
To doze . . .
— Only for that
I was not . . .
How much longer
Until dawn?
What's the good . . .
Slumbering on 'till dawn
Is more pleasant.
It is longer
Until our world . . .

About Winter   *De iarnă*

Hoarfrost,
Glaze frost,
People fall
On the street,
On the crust of ice.
No good walking
Without a grappling stick.
There is a painful laugh
Of falling
And hurting.
A beginners' waltz?
Or is everybody
Just drunk . . .

Newsreel *Jurnal*

Pan's pipes
Pagan
And fabulous,
Like a rush
Of centaurs.
Not for
The sensible . . .
Let us return in such a way
As to unbend
Through music,
Solemn and slow —
— 'God Save the King!'

Study *Studiu*

When I searched
For words
In dear dictionaries . . .
— Love
— Affection
— Beloved . . .
It was snowing
Or flowers were dying . . .
Years have flown . . .
There was also the word,
— Sympathy . . .

Peace *Pace*

And bored
By life's
Questions . . .
The answer —
Petty
And hasty . . .
Instead
Of sad tears,
It should be
Raining, quietly!
Much more,
And quietly.

Mythology *Mitologie*

You expect
From the horizon,
Countries
And seas,
Promises . . .
Playing
Innocently
In paradise.
Figurative?
Then, you run
From horizon to horizon,
With a ludicrous
Yell.

Cogito   *Cogito*

I have fulfilled
All my political
Prophecies.
I am content . . .
The sky
Is divine,
Clear
Or violent.
A famous
Aphorism
Helps you
To live . . .
It's neither tomorrow,
Nor today,
Nor yesterday —
The time . . .

Destiny *Destin*

A voice
From the past,
Sings sadly,
Just like you
It deludes —
To stay, and to think
Back to youthful times.

And if today
And also then,
It had also wept —
The whole field
Would be a flower,
The whole sky
Would be a smile.

Incident at the Ball *Incident la bal*

Do you remember?
The orchestra was roasting
The ball
In bizarre prophecies . . .
How I left that place
I'm not sure —
Or that you could have stayed
In that monstrous uproar.
I heard
Later
That it had ended
In a furore . . .
— The night, that night . . .
As from sinister centuries . . .

Evening   *Seară*

Silence . . .
Not one thing moving.
Yellow leaves, dry,
Red,
Ready to fall . . .
Behind the houses
The sun starts
To set.
Silence . . .
Not one thing moving.
In the yards a voice here and there.
Among houses,
Vivid and long colours,
Towards sunset,
Stealthily,
Slowly,
Haloes vanish . . .
Night.

In Winter *În iarnă*

Blue,
Red,
Mauve,
White,
You'll sleep, now
Abandoned flowers —
The white snow
Flows over you.
Even colder,
In the bed
At the back of the house.

Thoughts *Gândiri*

Beautiful
Merry
Good
Ugly
Sad
Bad,
Causes from eternity
And sociability . . .
With you I dreamt
In panoramas . . .
Somewhere, the sound
Of a guitar . . .
Ripe fruit was falling,
In a paradise garden.
Beautiful
Ugly
Merry
Sad
Good
Bad —
Causes from eternity
And sociability . . .

Chemistry   *Chimie*

Do you like it?
As from fermented products,
The homage
Of an inventor friend,
To become
An alter ego,
When you taste it alone.
What a transformation . . .
Only from this
Homage
Of an inventor friend.

Legend *Legendă*

— How well he wrote
And with talent
An inspired man
From the last century . . .
It has something of actuality.
Happenings,
Places,
Almost like today.
What an inspired man . . .
Or has the work suffered
Changes
Over time . . .
How well he wrote,
— But never spoke.

Pastel   *Pastel*

It is cold on the field . . .
There are still
Bits of snow.
Tiny flowers
In ditches.
Far off,
Young sun
Rushes . . .
Zephyr,
Azure.
It is cold on the field . . .

Libation *Libelă*

Unique
And sad
I stay with nature,
All beings
Are gone.
— You will be healthy,
Immortal . . .
Try the wine
From the vineyards,
To make the world return . . .

Twilights   *Amurguri*

Twilights
Dyes
Sad colours,
Unexpected pains . . .
Twilights . . .
Whitewashes
Cosmetics
So many times,
You bring
Contemporary thoughts,
To passing times . . .
Twilights . . .
Dyes
Sad colours
Whitewashes
Cosmetics,
Abandoned hopes . . .

Moment *Moment*

I

Since thought is at rest . . .
The prose of life is there
Watching . . .
Wasteland crossed
Mostly with screams
Of physical pain . . .
How they left
Those hopes,
How they left
Those longings . . . .
What a great man you were,
And so many have passed . . .

II

When silence besieges me
And I feel peace sustains me,
Life is a heaven, a pleasure —
There can't be better than that.
And if times bring sadness
To surround me once again,
Life will be a hell, repugnant,
There can't be worse than that.

On the Horizon   *În zare*

— There is a town
In the course of war,
From that waking moment
Until going to bed.
For more
Than bread,
Very difficult.
And who knows how
And when it will finish.
There is a town
With a deep sounding knell.

Late Verse   *Verset târziu*

At night silences
Of a tomb descend,
And gloomy whispers
Fly on the wind.

Wasteland and for centuries
You're not and I'm not there.
And the citadel is sleeping . . .
Nor is anyone else there.

Epode *Epodă*

Love, passionate past,
Purity,
The theorem of today . . .
Auroras with gold
And ruby on the horizon,
With fantasies of labour.
Days dawning,
Mornings full of summer
And a hard freeze —
Winter . . .
Romantic letters,
And suicides . . .
Love, passionate past,
The theorem of today.

New Year's Eve   *Revelion*

I

Pleasures wander,
Rich snow,
Gorgeous,
On Christmas Eve.
— Demijohns of wine
And years of gladness,
Whips snapping
As at other times . . .
Let's look in the mirror,
And the singing night
To send us to sleep
So as to forget.

II

Snowflakes
Among naked trees,
The sad sighs,
To snow up in drifts
The doinas themselves.
I stay alone,
And snowflakes,
Among naked trees,
Will entertain me,
With lily-white flowers
For they found me a grave.

III

Let's sing of me,
He who is me . . .
Stoned
At the year's end.

Years, years gone by —
Goes my song,
Years, years stay,
I meditate, drinking.

In the case of me drinking
For nothing in particular,
It is not a vicious circle
Nor is the wine vinegar,

My intention is
To do just this,
To go and get stoned
At the year's end.

At Edges   *În margini*

And as I was walking
On the bank of some water,
Fish swam downstream,
Dogs rummaged rubbish,
Crows landed on ruins,
In the silence of autumn..

Thus, there was water,
Earth and air
And only a deserted fire
Was still glittering
In the remnants of a flood plain
In the blue of evening.

Restorations *Restituiri*

Reading what I published
Many years ago:
Admirers,
Gossips
Past melodies,
Roses of childhood.
Socialism,
A mixing of languages,
Intimidation,
Enigmas of hazard,
Socialism . . .
I read what I published
Many years ago:
Past melodies,
Roses of childhood.

Fiefs *Feude*

Pink
Yellow
White
Green
Ash grey
Carpets
Landscapes on horizons:
The White Emperor,
The Red Emperor,
The Black Emperor.
Unctuous riches
In a distant hiding place,
Utopias
Mirages
Behind urban walls . . .
Creations of the mind.

Ideal Verse *Verset idéal*

A thought overwhelmed me,
No end to it —
A flow of melody
Dismissed it.

Then the flow of melody
Left me for ever more,
Thoughts of everyday,
Close in as before.

Prosaic Verse   *Verset prozaic*

Lately it is false,
Despite what one says,
Always to judge values
Of amazing technologies.

Outside there's wet
Thaw,
Eczema
And gonorrhea,
Those and many more, miseries . . .
And stunted aspirations —
But life's flow is also sweet . . .
Perennial spring . . .

Serenade *Serenadă*

A serenade of weeping . . .
The day of work is at an end,
For an evening of dreaming
They've sung the serenade.

The night slowly
Sends all in sight
To homes, to go to bed,
For an evening of dreaming
They've sung the serenade.

Good night!

Fantastic Verse   *Verset fantast*

A waltz
Wept at a distance . . .
Sometimes heard
At times of sorrows.

A demonic infinite
And bitter ironies,
Pains that were heard
In lonely shadows . . .

Slavic Verse   *Verset slav*

A much sadder tango
Was sung somewhere . . .
Let me drink,
This social gain
Instead of always
The same rotation
In the Universe . . .
Or a hoax . . .
If silence
Falls, again,
Every minute,
— Unhappiness . . .

Other Verses

Alte Versețe, 1899–1957

Contains poems not included in books, published in various publications (reviews, magazines, letters, etc.), from his debut until his death.

Rotten Autumn (*Toamnă putredă*) / 305
Falling Heavily . . . (*Cade larg . . .*) / 306
I Am Silent (*Eu tac*) / 307
I Fell Asleep . . . (*Am adormit . . .*) / 308
Bisyllables and Monosyllables (*Bisilab și monosilab*) / 309
It's Snowing (*Ninge* 'Ninge. Bolnav stau în casă . . .') / 310
Autumn Lines (*Rânduri de toamnă*)
    (Alternative title [Yes] [*Da*]) / 311
Who Is Small . . . (*Cine-i mic . . .*) / 312
Dialogue (*Dialog*) / 313
Who Sings . . . (*Cine cântă . . .*) / 317
What Can I Do? (*Ce să fac? . . .*) / 318
In a Byre . . . (*Într-o șură . . .*) / 319
Astonishing Snow . . . (*Ninge fenomenal . . .*) / 320
Like a Wine (*Ca un vin*) / 321
To a Clown (*Unui clovn*) / 322
Loneliness, I Didn't Want You (*Singurătate, nu te-am voit*) / 323
Dying Autumn (*Toamnă murind*) / 325
You Died . . . (*Tu ai murit . . .*) / 326
Autumn Nerves (*Nervi de toamnă*
    'Toamnă . . . iar sunt copil . . .') / 327
Love Song (*Romanță* 'Când luna e o roză de argint . . .') / 328

Blood, Lead, Autumn (*Sânge, plumb, toamnă*) / 329
Hebrew Lady (*Ebreia*) / 330
Verse Wandered Off (*Vers divagat*) / 331
To an Alcoholic (*Unui alcoolic*) / 332
And what . . . (*Și ce . . .*) / 333
Egypt (*Egipet*) / 334
Festive (*Festivă*) / 336
And if (*Și dacă*) / 338
My Friend the Fig Tree (*Prietenul meu, smochinul*) / 339

Rotten Autumn *Toamnă putredă*

Tragedy, misery, weeping . . .
Come in no particular order.
Life . . .
The music weeps for somebody.
One knows what a tremendous drama
Now careers across the white screen . . .

Falling Heavily . . .   *Cade larg . . .*

Snow falls heavily,
Falls sadly, like years,
Much more in vain.

It snows heavily in an ignorance
Of about two thousand years.

Over night white flowers fall . . .

And on the horizon of ice
No sign appears, none at all.

I Am Silent   *Eu tac*

I've been silent a long time, you, since yesterday . . .
Enormous violet horizon
On window, on brain, on bones:
>	Gale
>	Wail
>	Flail

>	Lock
>	Mock
>	Pock

>	Wept
>	Crypt
>	Slept

>	Poem
>	Dream
>	Again

On windows, autumn sounds
With leaves of metal . . .

I Fell Asleep . . . *Am adormit . . .*

I fell asleep at the stove
On Christmas Eve . . .
I fell asleep weeping . . .
On the frozen streets,
Wept lily-white flowers,
While silver jingle bells
Laughed in harmony.

Bisyllables and Monosyllables *Bisilab și monosilab*

Extract
Money
Bad
Empty
Flock
Gone
Put
Aim
Stupid
Tragic
Logic.

I was
Stupid.
Exist
Tragic.
Exist
Stupid.
What tragic
Logic.

It's Snowing   *Ninge*

It's snowing. I stay at home, sick
And factories send out signals
At dawn, noon-time, and night-time
That maybe I can no longer work . . .
In every passing woman
I think I see my loved one . . .
I can hardly shake the packets
For that last smoke.

Autumn Lines *Rânduri de toamnă*
Alternative title [Yes] [*Da*]

Yes, I walked on the streets you wrote to me about . . .
There is a grief of autumn there . . .
Round the hospital, at the barracks, it's sad, leaves fall.
In Court there was an interesting case . . .
Oh, and a few dried leaves flew into a book shop . . .

It is autumn, I would like to write you some verses . . .

In the public garden, a French alcoholic
Was smiling watching a bed of pansies,
On the roof of the music pavilion there was a raven,
I asked him about you but he didn't say anything.

It's autumn, everyone rushes, but it's so desolate . . .

Yes, a balance of trade still continues in town,
It's a little sadder, being that it's autumn —
I still haven't found anything,
I will write in more detail some other time.

Who Is Small... *Cine-i mic...*

Who is small and who is mighty?
No one's either small or mighty;
Each is how he seems to be;
Everyone sings, it seems to me...

Come on, onwards!

They're all, they're all words.
A rocking motion.
Come on, slower...
Yet even slower...
Anyway,
Haste is vibration.

Hora, hora...

It's the hour
For oblivion.

Dialogue   *Dialog*

— Shall I come?
— I'm afraid.
— Heh, see?
— (Oh, no) he's coming.
— Quiet.
— . . .
— I came (I'm here)
— Where . . . I don't see you . . .
— Near you.
— Quiet.
— Oh! . . .
— Oh! . . .
— How . . . I weep.
— I weeping . . . (me too)
— I am sick.
— We are . . .
— I want to sense you.
— I sense you.
— Off, off, what have I done?
— No matter.
— I lost you.
— I'm going mad.
— I'm going mad.
— How?
— How?
— It would be better then.
— Then.
— To the infinite.
— To the infinite.
— Yet how?
— How is everything.
— Who knows . . .
— Who knows . . .

— Poetry.
— Poetry.
— Let's go!
— Let's go!
— Where, where?
— Up.
— Up.
— Where?
— Where?
— Up on high!
— Up on high!
— Who?
— Who?
— It's higher.
— It's higher.
— Me, me, you, you.
— Smoke.
— Smoke.
— And . . .
— What was that?
— What can it be? . . .
— Poetry.
— Poetry.
— A cigarette.
— A cigarette.
— Oh, love.
— Oh, love,
— Shadows . . .
— Shadows . . .
— Coloured.
— Coloured.
— Dream . . .
— Dream . . .
— Come with me!
— Come with me!

— Where?
— Where?
— Who are these?
— Other shadows.
— Come to the sun.
— Come to the sun!
— Shadows...
— Shadows...
— Coloured.
— ...
— We are here in the room.
— Yes.
— What was that?
— Maybe, a dream.
— Ah!
— Ah!
— Do you want to go to bed?
— Do you?
— I'm going.
— I've gone.
— Ah!... I'm going to bed...
— Are you asleep?
— I'm still looking out of the window,
For I'm thinking of you
Near the sleepy bedside lamp...
— But I am still thinking of you
And my eyes hurt from lack of sleep.
— Ah! How many nights?
— Ah! How many nights?
— How are you?
— How could I be?
— I look at the night, and I see myself mirrored there.
— I don't think I'll go to Paris...
— I've been here a few days.
And I saw you on the street

And you saw me in your mind . . .
. . . A few metres behind.
It was late . . .
I felt you.
— Yes, something's at the back of my mind.
— Hey! I will go to Paris!

Serene, total:
From a game, subtle,
Ideal,
Serene, infernal.

Who Sings . . .   *Cine cântă . . .*

Who sings in a monotone?
Everything sings, and in tune.
It is muted
Tamed, tamed,
Harmony,
Poetry
And sublime anarchy . . .
And there is no affect:
Nobody's laughed, nobody's wept . . .

That's how it should be!

. . . A cigarette, smoking
And then back to dreaming . . .

What Can I Do? *Ce să fac?...*

What can I do?
Do a . . .
It is better with a flower — flower . . .
A flower — flower?

Someone sings in a flower,
Really?
Worker bees . . .
So it seems — so it seems,
So as to work their magic power.

A poet and a poetess,
Each to his own.
Then, nothing will come amiss.

In a Byre . . .   *Într-o șură . . .*

In a byre
The children again
Make a coloured star
Out of paper —
Dream of peace,
Of love,
For times
Foreseen . . .

Astonishing Snow... *Ninge fenomenal...*

Such astonishing snow...
As it used to be.
With a bizarre misery
The cold laughs miserably...
Oh, through the snowed up town,
Ravens fly randomly.
Past the houses,
With a bizarre misery,
The cold laughs miserably...

Frozen hard, all of it,
I walk on the silent streets...
Work and sadness,
Dream of peace, of love.

Like a Wine *Ca un vin*

I'll drink, what else to do?
Until test results, enjoyment's welcome.
Why should it be terrifying
When it's just a 'delirium'?

Ah! If you were the very essence,
Produced by repeated fermentation,
We would be closer to learning
About life's lamentation.

To a Clown   *Unui clovn*

Talent laughs sardonically
With noble aspirations.
There go, there go white clouds
On a sapphire sky.

When on the street someone
Slaps your face in reality
People laugh as if at a circus
Thinking it to be mimicry.

Loneliness, I Didn't Want You
Singurătate, nu te-am voit

Dreadful
Is the void of loneliness!
I am the one she killed . . .

Loneliness?
The burden of silences
Slanders
By sighs.

Loneliness . . .
Your eye
Stares frozen hard
At the eye of the thought
That's unshared . . .

Loneliness,
I never wanted you!
Cruel — life
Gave you to me.

You asked life
To make me
— Your prisoner —
Loneliness . . .

Everybody . . .
How they captured me . . .
Yet they
Never wanted me.

From the loneliness
Of life

Into the loneliness
Of death, nobody
Understands
This depth . . .

Poets, avoid
Loneliness.
Among people
There's life . . .

Dying Autumn   *Toamnă murind*

Autumn in the garden tunes its violin.
The chords weep sadly, long and prolonged
And into the empty room chords have thronged . . .
And weeping in the room, is also my violin . . .
All the chords weep long and prolonged.

The window is open . . . weeping are the violins . . .
Oh, it snows . . . and everything ends . . .
Pale, nervous autumn, has died singing . . .
My violin falls, and I fall tiring,
And autumn, the poetess, has died singing.

You Died... *Tu ai murit...*

In memory of Ștefan Petică

You died one of these days,
You, shy, blonde child of dreams, ever sad and missed,
But *She* still grieves, and calls you, gentle Christ,
Virgin in white, at a distance — does not believe the bad news.

The violins in mourning, with broken strings,
with the last trembling note, call out for you,
And in vain search the horizon asking for you
Virgin in white, with armfuls of withered roses.

Gone is the dreamer who was forever doleful,
And roses from now on will never ever bloom,
But will sleep in peace with the dead dream...
Virgin in white you will die on star-shaped marble...

Autumn Nerves *Nervi de toamnă*

Autumn . . . I'm a child again,
My confidence gone, I've lost it . . .
And again file off, crest-fallen,
The forgotten misery of those who knew it.
My heavy heart tumbles in bizarre cadences . . .
Consumption, autumn, and tatters . . .

For this, no, for that, no,
Leaves in the wind . . .
Ho! Ho!
I too was in this land,
Where did you go?

Again I am in the large town.
For those who disappear, nobody cares . . .
I dream . . .
Autumn . . . and twilights of sorrows
Stain all the public mirrors,
And murals with violet terrors.

Adieu, the dream hides somewhere . . .
In front? Behind? Anywhere . . .

Love Song   *Romanță*

When the moon is a rose of silver,
Come, I'll wait for you in a grove of silver.
If you can't come don't worry,
This century's tiny,
Everyone's a liar,
When all is traded for silver.

All that's left is the rose-moon of silver,
Today is not the time to pamper —
If you are not there
When I'm not there,
On the old bench you'll find
A lily
And a coin — of silver.

Blood, Lead, Autumn   *Sânge, plumb, toamnă*

Slowly through the sad rain
A coughing chest bent over
With blood on the kerchief again,
And went on round the corner,

Slowly through the sad rain.

All the wet lead of the fog here
Then diverts him and he weaves
Through the alleys of the square
And among the dried leaves,

All the wet lead of the fog here.

It is blood, lead and autumn,
With a black arm of peace
A branch keeps willing me on
Funereal and tenacious.

It is blood, lead and autumn.

Hebrew Lady *Ebreia*

Hebrew lady,
Weeping you set off from here in a large boat
And were caught, forever, in remote
America . . .

Hebrew lady,
With a longing for our country, with a yearning,
Watching over the ocean, you die weeping,
I suffer in the old continent.

Verse Wandered Off *Vers divagat*

I am with myself
Everything is at peace.
Poetry is outside humanity,
Far away
And in eternity.

Nice frames on paintings
Not for me such things . . .
What expensive clothing
And certain beings . . .
Ruling the world is not for me.

Poetry is outside humanity
Far away
And in eternity.
And times, times have passed.
Waiting for happiness is not for me.

To an Alcoholic *Unui alcoolic*

You stink of alcohol from afar
With so much fire and holler,
That if you blew in a pitcher of water
You'd change it into rachia.

And what... *Și ce...*

And thinking of novel ideas...
In the nightly noise of the town...
If, heavenly bodies spin around,
Or stay as far off sparkling stars...

Or after hard discussions abound
Inventions, sad or easy ideas...
And what if heavenly bodies do spin around,
Or stay as far off sparkling stars...

Egypt *Egipet*

I

Egypt — streak of life
In the country of unslept desert.
The Suez Canal —
A jewel enchained unjustly,
Oh, pyramids, why do death's locusts
Trouble your millenium slumbers?
Egypt weeps with pain's pearls . . .
Oh, cry no more, heroic Egypt!
The will of the times:
— Forward!
To the sorcerers of Dark Ages, I say:
— Let it blink
That serene eye over Egypt,
Never will the martyrs of justice die.

II

Egypt . . . overflowing Nile of gold . . .
Incest of Thebes,
Aurora of Memnon,
And devouring Sphynx,
Caravans of pilgrims and Bedouins
In the shadow of the pyramids.

Old echoes from there,
From the country of hieroglyphs . . .
Pyramids, the diadem of freedom
Laugh over your peaks —
Smile over the overflowing deserts . . .

Labyrinths . . . obelisks,
Boundless temples,

Mummies in the mystery of centuries,
Deciphering cartouches
With names of victors.

Snakes with magic powers
Secrets of olden times,
Civilization towards a future,
Heroes of freedom
Defend you . . .
Egypt, overflowing Nile of gold . . .

Festive *Festivă*

Pleasant evening . . .
Light of chandeliers . . .
And men taking my picture.

Oh, the hall with flowers
And my verses
So old!

I saw the golden riches
And silk of the past
And now Today's! . . .

Yes, I was in the castle
Of Nabobs
With crystals, mirrors and marble . . .

Look! I came like Hamlet
In my habit
Of mourning.

An old man of 75
With flowers and decoration,
I became a young man
Of just 57 . . .

Here, on my chest,
Is the star of Bacău . . .

I was a poem that
Night.

When the lights burn
In the centre
I am inclined to poetry . . .

The town is beautiful . . .
Full of Yellow Sparks.
Don't cry any more
That it once was sad!

Now it is the midnight hour . . .
Come for me to kiss you.
The wedding with white flowers
Has ended.

Acacias will tell the story!
Oh, mother,
Gentle mother,
Look at your son!

And if *Și dacă*

And if time brings back to me
Uncertainties that surrounded me,
A hell, my life is then disgust,
Nothing could be worse than that.

When stillness is around me
And I think that peace sustains me,
A heaven, my life is then pleasure —
Nothing can be better than that.

My Friend the Fig Tree *Prietenul meu, smochinul*

Love me, Marta, with a long caress,
Because
Today I saw my park powdered
By the cold frost of the Queen
With the cold lips,
Her Highness, Autumn.
The fig tree, my old fig tree,
Forgotten in the rusty
And
Long dilapidated
Park (cemetery of my first nostalgia)
Is weeping with the pain of broken branches . . .
On withered leaves bitter tears have appeared.
Oh, the tears, the held back tears,
Marta, my love,
The cruel nostalgia of my friend, the fig tree,
Stifles me . . .
O, Marta, my love and pain,
I hugged there — weeping,
My brother,
My friend,
My dear friend, the fig tree.
Destiny desired
Our souls to be entwined
To hurl their pearls in the mire.
Let us weep, sweet, dear friend.
Let us weep, defeated friend,
For our cruel pain . . .

Night Pieces

Bucați de Noapte 1926–1956

Prose poems

Late (*Târziu*) / 343
At the Coffee Party (*În cafeu*) / 345
In Vain (*În zadar*) / 347
The Black Cube (*Cubul negru*) / 348
When Leaves Are Falling (*Când cad frunzele*) / 351
Snow Storm (*Ninsoare*) / 353
The Thaw (*Moina*) / 355
A Novel from the Past (*Nuvelă din trecut*) / 357
Waves (*Valuri*) / 358

Late *Târziu*

In the rooms with open doors it is late ... There are neither pictures, nor old photograph albums, nor faded books, yet everything rests in silence.
I listen from the smaller room in the light of a lamp: Ah! If I could avoid shouting one word tonight ... and drop ...

I have forgotten who lives here, and where they have gone. It is late; on the streets there is the whisper of goodwill and of extreme suffering, or else nothing ... and the floor is old and the logs for the fire give you the sensation they are skulls; my mind keeps an unsteady pace of empty thoughts ... until a molecule is crushed in my brain, until everyone can say: 'See what you've done!'

Oh, later, later, after so much, the same things will look quite pleasant ...
And this night's tears will make no sense ... Oh! If I could avoid bellowing one word as terror grows — and drop ...

Why light the lamp now? The door is open, so is the window ... I sleep on my feet in the centre of the room, shaking in an abandoned darkness ...
Forgotten in the dark end of the room ... A dog pulls back angrily, barking; a cat leaps to the windowsill and retreats quickly backwards ...
I sleep on my feet in the centre of the room in an abandoned darkness ...
A cricket chirps in the silence ...

It's never been any different ... the sun always finds, standing here — a tired sentinel of despised loneliness ...

A cold, windy morning ... an empty room ... As one walks the floor creaks, the pen weeps on paper ... Perhaps it writes ... For what times?

For what reason? Dark clouds cover the window ... Wet fences and wood ... Dark clouds darken my eyes ... and it wants to rain again ... The clock has stopped ... It no longer wants to measure time ... Some money is on the corner of the table, and thought is closed ... The dark cloud stays at the window like a night of ice.

The bed is unmade and clothes wait upon the chair ... Perhaps it's late ...
I've stopped thinking about her ... Perhaps it's late ... And the wind
Slowly pushes the cloud from the window so as to replace it with another ...

It is night, the time when people go to bed and make love ... When all the town plays with notes of rain as on an old piano ... alone, through the house to compose verses ...

If the whole town plays like an old piano ... what is thought in itself?
Tomorrow we will go to buy a loaf of bread, a brown one ... Onwards ...

At the Coffee Party   *În cafeu*

An animal magnetism, deaf echo of an enormous wave of water, a long earthquake in the smoke of the coffee party, where each one in the crowd looks alike . . . It's a thought that crosses your mind as you turn your head,
Or see with tired eyes . . .

There was a sadness and a remote silence around a palace surrounded by an immense park, at the side of a country road . . . Summer scenery pulsing with sadness and silence . . . And there are small houses with clay floored verandahs, the roof larger than the house itself, and skeletons of slanting barns full of hay — or nothing.

When you are here, dusted under the sun, you see ladies in thin dresses
staring thoughtfully towards the lake.

Knowing you are a 'nobody', they laugh. The ladies move closer together, and one, with her tired hands upon another's shoulder, glances at the dusty visitor with narrowed eyes . . . Elegant on this summer's day they move off to walk along paths where fantasy is more plentiful.

At the buffet pavilion someone is serving ice-cream and beer — Oh, and be so kind as not to sign the album since they already know you are 'What's his name'.

The beer is good, the day melancholy . . .

Inside the palace there are objects d'art, and dreaming ladies who are avoiding large mirrors . . .

In other rooms people read or sleep . . .

At night he talks of leaving and takes the dusty road full of burdocks and dwarf elders, along old fences of osier and thorns.

Those who entertained the crowd have already left . . . I will sing alongside these walls on the open fields . . . No one about . . . The moon is a magnet and the night has no idea how I feel . . .

The wall surrounds the park with a kilometric silence that saddens the same as the cheap perfume of past times . . .

On the fallen foliage beasts rustle as they emerge into the full moon on the edge of the fecund and putrid lake . . . I sing like a large frog, when from bell-towers the resurrection tolls, and when sleepless cockchafers join the people called by the bells.

A thought flows like a woman of stone who sleeps, and a melody marks the abyss . . .

Within moments the moon has descended to the poplars. People walk about holding candles and I can weep slowly, loudly, in this night where nothing can be heard . . . I weep because this year the waltz is as sad as the old ones were, and because everyone was intelligent in that eating place.

In Vain   *În zadar*

Perhaps there was one circular night when we no longer knew each other, when all that was written was forgotten, when, starting from some point, one arrived back where one had started . . . A night, late to come, putting on that facial expression, that forgotten fixedness, forgetting possible beauty which perhaps many have forgotten.

In the rest all was vanity . . . And the moon tilted towards setting with a terrifying light above the town asleep under snow, reflecting itself on the many china photographs in the cemeteries . . .

I don't know who hung a bit of paper on a spider's thread, so that an all time solitude would sleep on these walls.

This late, late hour on icicles, on the distinguished ball in the echo of a band, in the hall of a palace . . .

There was the sadness of not mastering a foreign language so as to chat with the descending moon or with the passer-by squeaking the snow before dawn . . .
This late, late hour, like everything else for me regarding time, involuntarily I mistake a skull in the dark mirror . . . But you should never believe . . . A star was tiring my eyes and the street lamp was changing the face of the earth that was moving towards light. I would stand up from my old chair, from the mirror of frozen windows, in the night that still lingered . . .

So starts a new day . . .

The Black Cube   *Cubul negru*

Irritated by this long agony of a suspect century, humiliated more than ever by the ironical comment of a poet who belonged to the future era of beauty, I came home late at night, maddened by the misery and the lying in which I appeared.

I was lost, useless, more ridiculous than ever.

The small town slept in its night . . .

At home, as I lit the lamp, a white envelope appeared on the floor near the door, in the silence of the room where I lived long with never any letters from anyone.

I open the envelope and read on the black envelope, written in white:
'Come to the iron bridge. Tomorrow afternoon at three.'

I thought I wouldn't go, as on that night all real life had devastated me, I was indifferent to the invitation. To me it was a luxury, good for the bizarre emotions of others.

But next day I was at the bridge.

A gentleman and a lady in black led me quickly to a waiting coach.

The coach set off, the lady, smiling, put a mask upon my face through which I could see nothing.

When she removed it we were in a large sitting room, old but well lit.
Outside night had already fallen.

After a while each took a bath, scented, and wrapped only in large towels we returned to the room.

No one else was there and the mansion was sleeping ... It must have been past midnight ...

Our faces were pale and silent, and above us floated the disgust of a century.

Somewhat nervously they switched off the light, and in the deep darkness they opened a secret trap door in the floor of the room.

A square of light from the cellar, burst onto that corner of the floor.

With faint whispers the draped bath-sheets slid from us.

Today's real nudes ...

With her hair unbraided, she was the first to descend. We followed, and the trap door closed behind us.

A black cube of a cellar, upholstered in black velvet, surrounded us from floor to ceiling. No windows.

On the ceiling hung a bulb spreading violet light into this cube of forgetting, and in one corner a stove hidden from sight caressed our nudity with its softening warmth.

We lay back on the black velvet sucking in black aromas from three black glasses.

Our eyes gazed sympathetically, burning ...

"Sing!" he said.

And she took the black guitar and began with an ever softening voice that poem of Poe's . . . 'The Raven'.

The refrain 'Nevermore, nevermore' was fading, hardly whispered, when the guitar stopped . . .

We were drinking in black aromas from black glasses . . .

"Dance!" he said.

She stood in the pale, violet light . . . Oh, beauty of line showed natural obedience . . . She danced dreamily, lazily, decadently . . .

After a final spiralling glide she fell near us like a star in this black cube . . .

We were drinking in the black cube amid cigarette smoke and the bulb revealed the end of the century.

Now we were even more silent . . .

Suddenly, the light off, and the shadow of Karl Marx appeared in the night of the black cube with the help of a magic lantern.

A hysterical scream left their throats.

They gripped me with anxious arms and a shower of bizarre kisses sent us into a deep sleep in the black cube of forgetting . . .

The next day I was again led with the same mask on my face. At the same bridge we parted.

"Tomorrow we will leave for good", they said, and our century ended.

When Leaves Are Falling   *Când cad frunzele*

Thin rare trees with thin branches, with small leaves, yellow, they were there, solitary, on a calm day nearing Autumn . . .

On empty pathways, she was telling me how she liked perfume and powder. And even her powdered profile appeared clear, and her light blouse had a soft perfume.

"Ah. shoot me here in my left breast", said the lover, and afterwards, he shot himself the same way, and they stayed forgotten in the meadow by the town's waterside. Perhaps the drama in this newspaper happened in scenery such as this; What a love! What passion! What great feeling in front of such prosaic surroundings!"

"Yes," I replied, "It is interesting."
"Some fishermen found them during the night, notified the authorities . . .
It's almost a novel."

She went on and on, gazing in a mirror at her red lips and large eyes.

She could well be a refined lady, I said to myself, coming to forget her boredom in the park of empty pathways.

Among the trees, far off, a coach following us at walking pace.

I could make out something else from our surroundings that seemed narrow when wide . . . nobody, just her smile and silence.

The music ceased to play long ago around here, as well as lovers' meetings of which this lady spoke.

Oh the proud waltz . . . perhaps splendid . . . and the cool night when the trumpets wept in the park . . . Let me walk with you, like this . . .

Oh, poor prostitute . . . The night goes up and down. On the empty pathways we have walked enough. Novels have their ends.

She shivered with cold. She put her fingers to her lips as in a tender farewell and left.

Among trees, at a distance, the coach was taking her towards the town, leaving me alone to wonder whether I would ever see her again.

Snow Storm   *Ninsoare*

Outside the door jingle bells were jingling . . . and it was snowing.
In the night, the village was hidden. A soft echo and the snowing spread quiet and wide. I left with the party in full swing. Young ladies at the piano, dancing, food and wine. I was going to the other side of the village in the sleigh that belonged to a family attending the party, and I left to go to bed or stay awake. Covered by the fur blanket with a maid in another fur blanket next to me, we slid along the unseen streets hidden by snow.

Once there we climbed the steps to the verandah . . . The maid opened the door to the hall, lit a lamp and excitedly happy, did her best to please me.
Inside the room there was a green light from the icon lamp and a warm silence . . .

I rested on the edge of the bed and the girl entered another room through a door with bead hangings.

Throughout the night it snowed. From time to time one heard sounds of old iron door handles and creaking, then nothing. I was undressing in the green light, going over in my mind melodies from the party, swallowing a sob at my eternal estrangement. A horde of unthought thoughts kept me awake gazing through narrowed eyelashes at the bead drapes. A pale green cat entered slowly . . . looked towards my bed and leapt easily over me . . .

A bare arm moving aside the beads, unbraided hair, and the whole of the green girl was in my room. Through lashes I watched the stops and silent advances motionless, holding my breath and the desire to open eyes wide.

There are intimate beauties that remain for solitude. The snow continued sticking to the windows and the girl retreated slowly, the cat in her arms, undulating the bead hangings. Then a shadow lingered, looking back.

As if bored by everything, the green light began to extinguish itself, slowly.

A thread of emotions flared one after another... The bead curtains still moved slowly, but in vain.

One night... outside the door, jingle bells were jingling... and it was snowing... I was leaving... The green light could be seen through flakes of snow.

The Thaw *Moina*

As I had stayed home that day, bored by a young visitor, and since I couldn't ask him to go when it was so cloudy a day with watery snow that coloured the town a dirty black and white, I was thinking, without listening, and didn't know how to ask him if he would pour two cups of tea from the teapot on the window-sill.

My naivete in such matters was known even to children . . . Flattering admiration and stern observation mixed in disorderly logic. I had heard something similar for I knew many who were utterly defeated hoping for something or other . . .

After a while I managed to ask him to pour out the tea while I set about completing a half-finished manuscript for a review.

I'd been convalescing for some time, and forgetting the young man now busy with the tea, I was looking through the window, pen at rest, on that endlessly wet, weepy day. A young girl appeared at the window and the young man excitedly hurried to the door to let her in, inviting her out of the rain.

With a stifled nervousness she enquired about a street I'd never heard of before, but the young man told her it was far away and in a totally different direction . . .

There are moments, that a certain type of breathing, allows you to say nothing, but a catch of the eye suggests permission although truly, you disapprove. Busy with the manuscript and the determination to write, I overheard their intimacies . . .

The three of us drank tea amid a swarm of lies, at which I smiled, waiting for dusk to fall, to be alone once more to finish the manuscript, already beginning to bore me . . .

They left in the night. She, timid and indecisive; He, delighted as if having found a wonderful bargain . . .

But after they'd gone, I lost all concentration. Listening to the rain-snow life again seemed so frivolous. In vain, I searched for loneliness so as to describe it through the eyes of the defeated . . .

A Novel from the Past   *Nuvelă din trecut*

He who has ever stayed in a single room, by the light of a gas lamp late on, when one no longer knows whether the others are asleep or have left. When the blinds are lowered over the windows, he will read these lines to the very end.

For several days I have been browsing through a simple book with illustrations, all about a time gone by, and yet there were some pages I failed to understand. There was such an emptiness and, at the window, the trees thundered in the wind in the unknown night and over the silence of libraries I have known.

It seemed that the author, although legendary, was musing in the shade of the stove, wanting to explain what I didn't understand . . .

But there was a boring, slow-wittedness in the night.

I wanted to put out the light so as to end these winter feasts.

Oh, if only, you as reader, had not read these lines to the very end, for there were no past beauties to discover.

It was an indifferent night, with an ignorant contempt for the books I shall never find, with such descriptions I had known when a student with the help of a polyglot.

Ah, I had to listen to the music of farewells, and the small letters of footnotes that mentioned more old books, and the sandy rustling throughout the town of our times, And silence . . .

On well-known streets during the day, with the storm past, no one knows about my sleepless night or the place I'd just left.

Waves   *Valuri*

That's what was wasteland — She was calling me by waving tired arms, and I called her in the same way from the other side, on riversides separated across a wide stretch of water ... Our voices a moan over heavy and deserted waves — An echo of the last people under clouds of yellowed lead. From a distance a civilization was outlined in a profile of ruins, the earth awaiting radical transformation, and we were the last people across these waves ...

Oh, she was caught up by the arms of a monster and taken quickly to a far path into the shadow of cold forests ... And this woman had once bathed in clear water in the warm night and I had come to forget old indifferences in the shadow of the sleeping willows.

When I was suffering from stress, I saw her again one bright dawn, at the gate of the back yard leading to the river ...

Sleepy water and perhaps a fisherman, further off, perhaps a bird, some movement of colours, silence ...

If only she had travelled the world and in her eyes there had been a surprising night, and if she had kept telling me she had known me a long time ... I was looking at the garden crowded with plants, and on that free day I ate apricots and apples, growing damp with dew ...

I found her again one rainy night in a little room of a pub at the back of a yard, out of her mind, in front of a glass of beer, among the walls of tilted pictures, looking at me with the same night-eyes.

I was sitting, the night was passing. One could hear drunkards from neighbouring rooms. The lamp was blackening the pores of our skins, I was no longer myself, she no longer herself; and we forgot about the dawn and about the night. And the heavy waters were raining over us in the town with brooks and little bridges; And the night . . . The night was leading us into night . . .

Selected Prose

Proză Selectată

A Story I (*O poveste I*) / 363
For Sale (*De vânzare*) / 365
A Story II (*O Poveste II*) / 367
The Bear (*Ursul*) / 370
Little Old Grandmother Teaches Us a Game
   (*Ne-învață baba jocu*) / 372
The Tramp (*Vagabondul*) / 373
Bubi (*Bubi*) / 374
The Outlaw (*Proscrisul*) / 375
The First Blade of Grass (*Primul fir de iarbă*) / 376
The People (*Poporul*) / 377
Mother Hen with Chickens (*Cloșca cu pui*) / 378

A Story I   *O poveste I*

The children gathered in front of the hearth around the old man. He was sitting on a bench in a rough coat, legs crossed and sucking a pipe. From time to time, he would press the tobacco down and then add a small fragment of hot ember from the fire. They'd never seen him in such a good mood. He was laughing and joking, trying to scare the laughing children by clapping his hands in front of their eyes, or shaking one of them roughly in play.

The children sent up great hoots of laughter.
"Tell us a story, a story . . . . . . Yes, yes!" they all shouted. The youngest nestled up close to him while another sat on his lap. The eldest was behind him with one hand on the old man's shoulder caressing him, as one does to a child.
"Heh, are you going to tell us one?"
"Let's leave it for another time."
"Why?"
The youngest child pulled the pipe out of the old man's mouth.
"Give me my pipe back . . . "
"I'll give it back if you tell us a story . . . " and he ran through the house with the pipe in his hand.

He ran round and round the house a few times and the others followed. One of them caught him by the ear while another pulled the pipe from his mouth.
"You scamps," shouted the old man.

The children gave him back his pipe.
"So are you going to tell us a story or not then?"
"No"
"And why not?"
"Because I don't know any!"
"You always say the same thing . . . 'No's' only a word . . . you'll tell us anyway!"
"No, I'm not going to tell you one."

For some time the children thought about how they could find a way to persuade the old man.

"Heh, are you going to tell us one?"

"No!"

"No!" exclaimed the eldest... "Then... give us the pipe back", and he pulled the pipe out of the old man's mouth and began running to the door...

"Don't give it back to him!" shouted the children. Everyone was clapping hands in glee. The old man looked at them. "You scamps, you've got me now. Hi, then! Let's have a story..."

* * *

Published in 'Adevărul' 10.09.1903

For Sale   *De vânzare (Schiță)*

He was only as tall as half an arm.
The very old man raised him up, put him on his shoulders, and took a few steps around, shouting:
"For sale, for sale!"
The child laughs and claps his hands. Then he takes the old man's fur cap from off his head and with his tiny hands strokes the head of grey hair . . .
"Look, my hair is much, much darker here." — and he points to his bit of black hair.
"I'm an old man and you'll be one day . . . "
"Gee up . . . "
And he jumps from the arms of the old man running to one side. The grandfather smiles, looking at him affectionately, goes up to him and takes him by his hand.
"What's the matter? Are you upset?"
"Yes, I am."
"Heh! Let's make friends."
"I don't want to."
He puts one finger in his mouth and looks down.
The old man looks at him, then puts a hand in his pocket and takes it out pretending he has something in it.
"Take it."
The child looks away sidewards and smiles slightly.
"You haven't got anything there."
"Yes I have."
"And what if you haven't?"
"You can slap me."
"Really?"
Laughing, he comes over to the old man, who stretches out his fist. The boy catches it and tries to open the fingers. The hand is empty.
"There you are, I told you so!"
"Give me a slap then."

And the old man offers his cheek.
He hesitates a moment, looks at the wrinkled face of the old man and at the white beard. He steps slowly towards him and then hurls himself into his arms.
"I can't, I can't, you are an old person."
The very old man hugs and lifts him up, then walks around shouting:
"For sale, for sale!"

Published in 'Adevărul' 01.10.1903

A Story II *O poveste II*

The old man took his pipe out of his mouth and held it between his fingers. The children made a circle round him. He took the youngest one onto his lap, whispering 'little scamp!' and started the story.

"Once upon a long, long time ago. Such a long time ago that now it's just a story. There was an Emperor who lived in a far, far away land. He was rich, this Emperor, so rich that if the whole world was to put its wealth together, it would only be a quarter of what he had. He was an honest ruler, so honest that whoever came to him was given justice and when he left, he would praise the emperor to the heavens. However he wasn't happy, because he lacked something that usually brings happiness: He had no children. He was alone with his Empress in that rich palace. He would look at his unequalled riches and tears would spring into his eyes because he was wondering who would inherit it all. Then he would look unkindly at the Empress.
"It's all your fault!"
"No, it's yours!"

In this way they tossed the fault from one to the other every morning and every evening. One morning the Emperor was sitting alone in the garden when he felt a light hand touch his shoulder. He turned round and saw the Empress, happy and smiling.
"Your Highness, I had a strange dream," she told him.
" I too had a dream," he replied.
"What about?"
"You tell me first . . . "
"It fills me full of joy. I dreamt that from my head a flower grew. It was a very plain-looking flower yet it smelt wonderful, and the scent was everywhere — all around me . . . "
"My dream was just the same," interrupted the Emperor.

"What could it mean?"
They called the wise men of the court to explain it to them, and one of the elders said:
"This means that your Empress will give birth to a child. The scent means that he will grow to be a wise man, but he will be very plain-looking, and I don't want to hurt the Emperor's feelings, but wisdom always wears plain clothes. And that's what happened.

....

The younger child took the pipe from the old man's hand and pushed and pushed it into his mouth. The old man pressed down the tobacco, lit it with an ember, and gave it a suck. Then he spat out on the floor and went on:
"Well, well, a number of years have gone by and the news has spread all over the world about the son of the Emperor who was called Justice. He had the habit of sitting in the palace garden where he would teach justice and the people came from far and wide, and in the whole country there was never any injustice. It was the country of justice. The Emperor and the Empress feasted their eyes on him. They would hug and kiss him all the time.

Then he reached his 21st birthday. One day Justice was sitting in the garden waiting for people to come to be taught and he wondered why nobody came. The same thing happened on the second day, and the third, and each day after. So he sent messengers to find out why.
"They've found someone else." Answered the messengers.
"Who?"
"A handsome man who teaches them about pleasure. You taught them moderation and now they say they're fed up."
Justice stood still quite stunned.
The next day he went along too. He found Pleasure (for that was the man's name) sitting on a golden throne preaching to a crowd. The crowd was listening and drinking in every word he spoke.

"Go away from here!" shouted Justice. All the people turned to look at him.
"Don't listen to him," he shouted again, but the crowd turned back again to Pleasure remaining spellbound by his smile and then — crowded towards Justice hitting out at him. After this, Justice became very ill and died in that place. The Emperor could not stop weeping and the Empress died of grief. The whole world wept for Justice.

....

The grandfather's story had ended. The youngest was asleep with his head leaning on the old man's chest. The others were standing gazing at him . . .

Published in 'Adavărul' 05.11.1903

The Bear *Ursul (Schiță)*

Motto: Present day education

Laughter, guffaws of laughter, and clapping of hands.
The Boyar is sitting on the bed, swinging the child by the armpits. The mother stands, arms folded, looking on, and laughing.
"Up and down, up and down."
The child repeats after his father and bursts into great chuckles. Then he runs through the house, hides under the bed, bangs his feet on the floor and leaps out. He comes back with eyes sparkling with joy. In one hand he has a stick and in the other a rope which he can hardly drag after him.
"What have you got there?" Shouts the mother warning him with her finger. He jumps around about chanting "A bear! A bear!"
The father stretches out his hands and catches him.
"What do you mean, a bear?" he asks him.
"What do you mean, a bear?" asks the mother.
He laughs and keeps on shouting:
"A bear! A bear!"
"Let's go and see," the parents say one after the other, "Show us it then!"

Inside the house, the father and the mother wait impatiently, on hot coals.
"Come on, show us it then, crazy one," says the father.
"Another crazy thing."
"He is so clever!" adds his mother.
Somebody kicks at the door with feet. The door flies open.
"Oh!" they both exclaim.
The child appears with a stick in one hand, while in the other he holds the rope on the end of which is Caesar — a big dog with long ears, a hunting dog.

The father leaps up.
 "No, no, you musn't do that."
He comes close and caresses him.
"Hi!" he shouts. " The bear!"
"Let him go," the mother implores.
"You're not allowed to do that. I know I've many hunting dogs, but you can't do that, dear."
The child keeps shouting "The bear!"
"Stop it!" The father says suddenly. "I'll give you a much better bear to play with," and he hurries towards the door, shouting, "Alexander! Alexander!"
"Oh, yes!" Exclaims the mother.
The servant appears. Laughing, the master says, "Make yourself into a bear."
He in his turn gives a forced laugh. He bends down. The child puts the rope around his neck. The servant crawls on four legs making a growling sound, "Grrr! Grrr!"
And everybody in the house is laughing and clapping hands.

Published in 'Adevărul' 31.12.1903 when aged 22

Little Old Grandmother Teaches Us a Game
Ne-învață baba jocul (Schiță)

Little old grandmother was sitting on the covered terrace enjoying the children's game. They were trying hard to play it as she had taught them. They were also laughing as they went wrong, laughing in great outbursts and turning to look at the old woman.
"May you be lucky!"
The children let go hands and came over to her.
"Little old grandmother is teaching us the game." Shouted the children. She folded her arms across her chest and laughed lightly. "What, have you forgotten?"
"No, but tell us once again."
And one of them knelt before her and took her wrinkled and trembling hands in his small palms, caressed her brow as he spoke pleadingly. "Please teach us the game again."
"Show us just once more," said another putting his arms round her neck.
She shook her head. "No, I'm too busy," and she stood up.

The children joined hands again and made a ring.
" Come on, won't you teach us?"
"No, I'm going," and slowly the little old grandmother went a few steps and the bent body tilted over at each one she took. The children stood watching her leave. They broke hands in one place and laughingly went in front of her, then joined hands again but with her in the middle. Then they went into hoots of laughter.
The old woman in the middle was laughing too as she watched them.
"You giddy lot! Who could possible tell you off?"

The Tramp   *Vagabondul (Schiță)*

Night: a velvety vault spread with the dust of stars.
The tramp is alone with his paniers over his shoulders. His body tilts as he moves each foot. His lips tremble with hunger, and his eyelids keep closing from lack of sleep.
And yet he sees something in the distance. A ray of hope that lights the meandering of the road.
An escape?
"It is death."
His soul will fall as if to an abyss. Then he will feel nothing, nothing.
Then?
"Peace, silence, happiness."
Yet there will be one less in the world. One star less in the immensity of the stars spread across the vault.
The vagabond looks up at the vault. The stars are twinkling. A star is falling and the darkness left behind it covers the light of neighbouring stars.
The vagabond shivers and continues on tilting from side to side and thinking of himself and the falling star . . .

Bubi *Bubi (Schiță)*

The Mother sits near the window watching her daughter, small and agile as she jumps lightly upon the dog and puts her hands around his neck. She climbs up easily onto its back and puts her head against his neck stroking it.
"Bubi, Bubi . . . "
The dog stands there turning to look at the girl and wagging its tail.
"I'm going to show you my doll, Bubi."
And she ran off into the house.
She comes back with a doll in her arms, holding it close and kissing it.
The dog jumps up. She kneels in front of him and puts the doll close to his muzzle.
"Kiss it!"
The dog licks it.
"Sooooooooo!" she said spreading out the word. "Look, Bubi! You've got to love her too."
The mother at the window laughs out loud.
The child turns suddenly with the doll in her arms, frowns and wails. "Why are you laughing?"
The mother doesn't answer but goes on laughing.
"Then, there you are!" And she throws the doll down.
"From now on I'm not yours anymore. You can have your doll back!"
And angrily she jumps back on Bubi, putting her arms around his neck petting him
"You're not to love the doll anymore. It's mother's!"

The Outlaw *Proscrisul*

Outside there is a blizzard and it is pitch black. The two poplars in the yard are bending their peaks in the power of the wind.
The outlaw stops in the middle of the room, thoughts pile upon thoughts.
He sits at the table thinking.
Lovingly he seems to perceive a corner of land and sky . . .
How sweetly, how mildly it smiles at him. He closes his eyes.
Now he is alone like a fir-tree on the top of a mountain and is bending under the burden of his destiny.
But an outlaw should be strong, even stronger than a rock. He must never allow himself to cry . . .
Nostalgia!
He stays dreaming and sees his people whom he loved so much.
Slowly, from the centre of them all a figure of an angel opens out with big blue eyes, cleaving the space with his glance and looking gracefully and deeply into his eyes.
And now? The outlaw covers his face with his palms and cries.

The First Blade of Grass   *Primul fir de iarbă*

The first blade of grass, the first rocking leaf on a twig, the first chirping of a swallow is the spring of thoughts and ideals. A transparent air, a clear sky, blue into the distance, the far distance where it lands slowly upon the earth.
A flock of cranes glide in the heights.
Up there, up there, even higher! My soul rises there, there in clear spheres, like an eagle and from there my eyes embrace the whole world.
Oh! Nature sends you to sleep, yet never sleeps itself.
It is mild, sweet, caressing like the Doina which slowly, easily, flows, flows, thaws itself along with the heart of humanity.
No need to put effort into man's dreaming: towers upon towers, castles upon castles, proud and tall, rise up of their own accord.
Look! When the descending flocks come with their bells clanging — May they be damned! — it spoils everything and recalls raw reality.

The People *Poporul*

They had shattered the world.
The earth seemed a tree shaken by a sudden gale. The crowd had moved and the trunk of the tree was powerfully shaken. The branches threw off their leaves; in the chaos there was noise and . . .
. . . he was there in front of them all.
But the gale was like the gale, beginning with a small wind, it grew and became unchained; then became slower, and slower, until silence.
The chaos becomes clear and the sky is a limpid blue.
He is now alone and in chains.
He moved his body, the chains rattled and their rattle reminds him of past glory. Glory ? — it is like . . .
Now, when the crowd is lifting its head, wide eyed, watching the scaffold . . . he smiles towards the people and with a heart full of joy, because they watch him as he moves forward . . . The head falls, the blood flows.
The people who once shattered the world now leave quietly.

Mother Hen with Chickens   *Cloșca cu pui*

The street had nicknamed her Mother Hen with chickens, for she had five children and all of them went everywhere with her. The youngest she held in her arms. One of them held on to her skirt, another was at her side and the last two alone in front.
"Good health to them! But they're always hanging onto me."
She said entering the Priest's house one day. The Priest's wife folded her arms across her chest with wide-open eyes, then she narrowed them looking through her eyelashes and smiled.
"You see Mother, if you get them used to it . . . "
And she got close to the eldest and pinched his cheek. Then she pushed his fringe back and stroked his brow. "Long life to them, Mother!"
"God protect them against the Evil Eye," added the mother, sitting on the bed. She put the youngest alongside her and the Priest's wife gave her a stale bread offering. The child tried to chew the hard crust with the line of white teeth under his red gums.
"The bread's too hard for them — may they have luck —" said the mother in a sigh. And buttoned up her blouse, pressed her breast and then added looking at the Priest's wife, "This devil of a boy even sucks my blood."
"Heh! You knew what you were doing. You wanted it or you didn't want it, now you have to manage."
"Yes," the mother sighed loudly.
The priest's wife sat on a small stool in front of her and looked at the four children who were flicking through a Holy book of Psalms found on the table and then winked at the child on the bed.
The mother started to tell her of all her troubles and the Priest's wife from time to time put in a 'There! There!'
"Priest's Lady, I came here specially to see you."
"Why?"

"Well, it's just a small thing. Could you give me a cup of flour?"

The Priest's wife pretended she hadn't heard and interrupted her.

"Look Mother, times are hard and the Priest is ill."

A shriek of 'Mama!' interrupted the conversation.

The one on the bed had been trying to reach the cat and had fallen off. The mother picked him up.

"Look Mother, the child is sleepy. Why don't you go and put him to bed? Stop crying now. Be quiet. What a noise!" And she gave him a light tap.

The mother held him tight to her chest.

"Take him home and put him to bed," the Priest's wife repeated.

"I'm going, I'm going," and she stood up then added slowly, "but the cup of flour?"

The Priest's wife frowned. "Upon my word Mother, I haven't any. Heh, Mother the times are hard, extremely hard and the Priest has not received his salary."

And then quickly:

". . . but see your child has fallen asleep in your arms. Go and put him down," and she led her towards the door with her arms still folded across her chest.

The Mother pushed the children in front of her.

"I will put them all . . . " She added leaving.

Final Considerations

Dictated to his son, Gabriel between 1954 and 1957

- I'm writing nothing more.
- One can hear the echo of hate and drunkenness from others as well.
- One day I met myself, but I substituted myself for a friend.
- Is silence mute or melodious? It is called loneliness.
- Coins are beautiful; they consume themselves just once for one person.
- I've only had fleeting doubts over those precious human norms.
- A short song says much. A diluted one could be too long.
- There are boughs torn from Heaven.
- Some questions should not be reproved.
- The mind has plenty of time to play.
- Before reaching truth in this world, there are many directives.
- I no longer write anything that would be the equivalent of a coffee for the heart.

1955

- Once upon a time I too existed.
- Was I once a star in the sky? What am I now?...
- Am I the star? Could I light a wasteland?
- I would like to rule over the Sahara... I could light the silence...
- After such times why shouldn't I leave?
- If I ever existed, it was because I loved you...
- Has Agatha left? A fair star was my dream... But 'the red flowers have died'.

- Oh, good one, you work while I sit! ... The balance has crumbled ...
- How? Is my song crumbling?
- I kept on fighting, in a limited circle ...
- Shut up, sorcerer! If we perish not even bears will tear us apart.
- My prophets? None ... Again there is sadness upon earth ...
- Oh, forefathers who have toiled on the fallow soil of life, George, Virginia, Ecaterina, Lina ...
- When Jesus died, not even Rome was ruled by Augustus.
- I confessed to the earth about my death ...
- I understand the word. It gives pleasure to the shiny stars ...
- Our century lifts towards the stars ...
- I said to the earth: silence ...
- George, stop your way towards destiny ...

1956

- You gather what my thoughts can still sow.
- Shakespeare? The mute sighs of London.
- My star, my little star, shall set too!
- When Mother Hen calls, I'll join her chickens.
- Why would Zeus care for me?
- And, yet, even today the sky vault sieves knavery over the world! ...
- When you know all the knavery, bitterness settles even if you don't want it to.

Final Considerations

- My childhood has passed, for many, life is in disgrace . . .
- The present wants to knock me down, but it won't be able to . . .
- We all are rascals; we can't tell a wild apricot from a normal one.
- Bakonsky, let Cicerone speak about me.
- George is dying from life's painful bullet.
- I, myself have a legend, just as Bacău has one.
- Only the sky is free, the signs of my death are not yet seen.
- I no longer believe in Zeus, because Zeus is blind with the rest of us.
- Oh, meetings in life are short! 'Ad finis' this is what I want.
- If common sense comes into your head, don't lose it! It is a function of your brain.
- The essence of life? Don't be too essential!
- Bacovia, you will set!
- George Enescu, play your wonderful fiddle, soul of the country's soul.
- My major star, how much white hair you have given me!
- September . . . Oh, September, like a gold dumpling, a martin . . . Has it already died? . . .
- Here is the last echo of George Bacovia, which you should perceive.
- To work! . . . No lazybones, you blockheads, to work! . . .
- I appreciate Cik Damadian. I like how he drew me in *Contemporanul*.

- We go too far in searching the past. It is the present I long for.
- How I sang in my *Scinteia* and the sparks kindle today.
- Ivesti... Ivesti... Stefan Petica... the handsome and beloved poet...
- A limpid YES, a dark NO, that is life.
- My life has been a love of mine, with perfidious tears...
- I like *Gazeta literara* very much.
- A blue eyed poet... Stefan Petica...
- You come too, muse of my last litanies... Come, muse, industrious star, welcome...
- What a crepuscular silence we have today!
- Behold the beauty on the vault of God — the poet who has never decorated himself with roses.
- I have trouble with the centre of my eyes... maybe this is the end...
- In stillness there is nothing... silence...
- Pamfilica Seicaru?... A scoundrel, he erased himself abroad like a traitor.
- Such is Gabriel. When he has, I haven't; when I have, he hasn't...
- Even the river Ganges flows towards the East...
- Oltenita Road — Argezi! Giurgiului Road — Bacovia; here there starts the social comparison...
- Beethoven's *IX-th Symphony*? It enchanted me so much; my ears feel so strange. Laurels upon laurels...
- In the shadow of Bacovian streets you find traces of love...

Final Considerations

- Look how beautifully I caught Argezi's sounds; he was looking for me later, but I had gone by then ...
- I still want golden wings.
- I was born in the worst days, with thoughts of lions, with a serenade to work ...
- Socialism is my friend. Let me have a drink in its honour, as at the lions' bridge ...
- Let the gentleman sleep; that gentleman is me, you, he, we, all of us ...
- Let us artists love each other: I love George Enescu as a great violin player, which is what he really is ...
- *Alexandria* is a book I would like to re-read.
- My brain woke up and said: 'I love life'.
- My body is emaciating and waiting for death ...
- My verse is almost fragile and delicate ...
- From selfishness to reality ...
- I greet destiny. I have seen the abundance of the century.
- Oh, Death, your clock is the silence ...
- Have a rest, my good one, you work for all of us ...
- Sometimes it rains upon the plain, rhymes one just cannot explain, sometimes it rains upon the peaks, and many things Bistrita speaks.
- I became old and sad on this Earth so as to see the Morning Star from Bacău ...
- The Earth is like a snake, the atom taught him not to bite.
- Calvary would not have existed had there been no humans ...

- When people start to slaughter one another, then neither Bengal tigers, nor African ones appear cruel.
- Gabriel, reading is a vice, but does not harm body or mind.
- Gabriel, why don't you go to bed? Do you still want to make notes? . . . Oh, my dream, I shake when I'm speaking . . .
- Better get drunk by the liquor of the mind than by the liquor of the devil.
- Don't be mean with your mind; give it good sweets and little quinine . . .
- Don't move away from books! Read equally good and bad books, so you can compare the good with the bad . . .
- An autobiographical preface and a photograph help one to better understand the author.
- A coffee and a cigarette, products of peace.
- Material drunkenness brings that which is spiritual . . .
- George Bacovia's poems shall appear again . . . many years out of print . . .
- Glory has not yet died . . . It still comes to her poet . . .
- I was faithful to poetry and wine . . . both friends of heavy silences . . .
- My verses wandered on the hard waves of twilight.
- I received the waters and leaves of my borough in rhymes . . .
- I sent to poetry the luminaries of joy . . .
- My luminary? A luckless star . . .
- Emptiness has just opened and is dragging me towards the depths . . .

Final Considerations

- Ferocious is the emptiness of solitude . . . I am its mortal victim . . .
- The void of empty spaces, of deserted existences . . .
- Solitude is the burden of silences torn off by sighs . . .
- Solitude, your eye looks icily into the eye of unrequited thought.
- Solitude, I didn't want you . . . Wicked life offered me to you . . . You asked for me from Life . . .
- Solitude, I am your prisoner . . .
- Poets, avoid solitude, life is among humans . . . How much I loved them . . . But they didn't want me . . .
- From the solitude of life to the solitude of death . . . and no one understands this depth.
- Oh, Gabriel, it is better to disappear with everything I've written . . . It is time . . . It is the opportune moment . . .
- I was a phenomenon from birth . . . superior to other humans and simple.
- I like the glory that withered . . .
- George you shall go to Green Emperor's star . . .
- I am a poet . . . to disappear, that's what I'm expecting . . . To society, I leave nothing on this earth . . .
- When I was brought into the world, the Gods whispered: you will be already life-weary!
- And I will soon pass like colts in stories . . .
- The stars in Bacău were yellow . . . Adieu . . . at night I meditate and keep silent . . .
- Gabriel I have known Bacău since those long passed years of departing youth . . .

- What was Bacovia other than a name throughout the universe...
- Here comes the spring and no flower will delight me...
- A silence came down upon my soul... Don't cause disorder in my life...
- I go to the realm of Dumitru for good...
- Children, play as long as time allows...
- Even the Pole star of night strengthened me during the day...
- Bunches of forget-me-nots? Do the Gods still love me?
- What am I besides a nest for a heart?
- Inside the house a gift... and money... and abundance...
- Yes! Again Berlin wants to be the muzzle of Europe.
- The London-Paris agreements? Every day brings a dose of poison...
- As to the problem of peace, if it stays in London, poor peace will stay covered in fog...
- America? How can it reach here? Won't the Pacific Ocean swallow it?...
- How am I? I just stay in darkness and watch the luminaries of the cigarettes in the mirror...
- I am thinking of the luminaries of peace... When do they rise, when won't they no longer set?
- Even the hoopoe bird when it looks in the mirror thinks it is a Polar star...
- For the large masses I was kept in darkness... Today I start to be known... Tomorrow?...

Final Considerations

- It is hard to say Bacovia... Today I am unknown. Tomorrow I am dead... and hidden...
- I wanted to write about beauty... a long time ago... today I do write, about what? I don't know any more...
- In poems of *Plumb* (Lead), I am unsurpassed...
- All scissors have a destiny: to spoil literary works.
- I made a colossal mistake to be born in this century...
- Jesus was great when he started a revolution...
- I regret that the Gods did not consult each other about me, Gheorge Bacovia ... to find my strength...
- Even when we see ourselves in the mirror as a hoopoe, we think we shine like a Polar star.
- Once upon a time there was a famous prince, He: Eminescu... Today he is dead, but his eternal writings are even brighter than rubies...
- Admiration... interminable applause, and then I saw myself in shop windows... but now I am in my room all by myself...
- Ah, Mirror, I am disgusted, for you tell us all the secrets...
- Life? A package of tobacco with an aspect of gold and a taste of metal...
- I haven't written much, but I described many things in my thrifty and concise way of writing...
- O, we write in vain... O, Gabriel. The rains have come and there are many vanities...
- Not working is a stupid sensation: it is like an over extended sentence with painful accents...
- I that time I was the caricature of ballrooms... I don't want to remember...

- I am the natural child of your epoch... Poets, don't write for ballrooms...
- The skirts steal our sight, let us not lose our minds...
- Oh, mother, what a pity I am alone and you are no longer at my side...
- Destiny, I don't like your kiss!... It is too bitter...
- Adieu, Bacău, you educated land... I live In Bucharest...
- One doesn't find equality in life...
- Destiny, I've seen you charming people... You never liked me...
- I am an apprentice in the barber's shop of life, for some people I brush with the broom of sorrow the traces of pleasures of the present...
- Is the present dead? Has the future gone? Is the past coming to life? For whom?
- Nothing about the poetess Agatha Grigorescu-Bacovia? This should be a topic for thought for the State Printing House.
- There is no serious study written about George Bacovia, even in "Mica Biblioteca Critica"...
- The young A. Baconsky is the only one who wrote really thoroughly about me in *Colocviul Critic*...
- Memories... Night... twinkles of stars... soon I'll be among them...
- I am always good to fill an empty space for a publisher...
- Jebeleanu and Cicerone, you are my children as well as Gabriel...
- How lonely I felt then in this world! 1916! Bacovia, the poet of 'Lead'...

- I wrote poems when the shoes were of gold and silver, and * 'opinca' of 'ogheli' . . .
- I said to myself: Life, I'll not be drinking for long from your fountain . . .
- Why do you stay in the dark? There's no madness to see . . .
- My brain no longer helps me to use that talent of the past . . .
- Angel of suffering, either you are dressed in white, or black, the world overtakes you . . .
- Put your foot on the threshold: Onwards . . .
- We shut our eyes and our life ends.
- Choose your friends my son: avoid flatterers who kiss you on your face and then, behind your back wash themselves with Eau-de-Cologne.
- Among the heavy waves of twilight, my verses also wandered . . .

1957

- Realities produce real effects on me.
- Pleasant night . . . Light from chandeliers and photographs. They filmed me. That night there was real poetry . . .
- Oh, the room full of flowers and my age old verses . . .
- I have seen the riches in the gold and silk of the past and of today . . .
- How poor we are, darling, how could you stay with me! . . .

---

* *Peasant sandals*

- I was in Nabobs' palaces. With crystals, mirrors and marble . . .
- And the two great ones seemed to embrace.
- Argezi, I love you, I enjoy the honour of receiving you.
- That night was a real poem . . . Don't you go to bed ? . . . No . . . My eyes are still good . . .
- The night is at the cross. Come to have a kiss! The wedding with white carnations has ended . . .
- From now on auroras will no longer come to me.
- When the lights are on in the town, I feel inclined to poetry . . .
- If only the past years had been tears . . . If only the past years had let us read twinkling stars . . .
- Old age cannot be proud . . .
- Tales from the past . . . Oh, come for a kiss, my Agatha . . .
- What do you expect, it is my brain: it thinks when it is not needed, and stays put when it shouldn't stay.
- The thought thinks the thought, and the thinking becomes ether . . .
- I am my own God and judge.
- O, non existent and too solitary a genius . . .
- George Bacovia, a buried artist and at the same time, eternal.
- Are all gone? Am I alone again? And Agatha is late . . .
- Shit! And what if my teeth have fallen out? This is a syncopation of life.
- A pink wave of consumption passed through my body, and life slowly flows out.

- Chandelier of my life, you have a few arms left . . .
- What a sadness. Camil Petrescu has gone too, early today.
- The rooster sang for him for the last time . . .
- What a pity! You are gone, my good friend.
- Hero of work . . . you died in the eleventh hour; you died still young . . .
- How soon am I going to go? . . .
- What a delirium is in my mind!! . . .
- You leave your family, friends, you dress in black silk, and like Jesus, you carry the cross . . .

Doi dintr-o lovitură

Poetry Index in English Listed Alphabetically

A

A Ballad (*Baladă*) (A night of sea-blue . . .) / 154
A Ballad (*Baladă*) (In the monastery . . .) / 211
About Art (*De artă*) / 237
About Winter (*De iarnă*) (A corpse, a raven . . .) / 175
About Winter (*De iarnă*) (Hoarfrost . . .) / 272
About Winter (*De iarnă*) (How fast it snows . . .) / 115
About Winter (*De iarnă*) (In lamenting echoes . . .) / 117
A Lake-Dwelling (*Lacustră*) / 43
A Legend (*Legendă*) / 204
Alone (*Singur*) / 94
Although Nothing (*Deși nimic*) / 244
Among Walls (*Între ziduri*) / 130
Ancient Twilgiht (*Amurg antic*) / 64
And All (*Și toate*) / 206
And if (*Și dacă*) / 338
And it's Snowing . . . (*Și ninge . . .*) / 124
And what . . . (*Și ce . . .*) / 333
A Night (*Noapte*) / 99
A Picture of Winter (*Tablou de iarnă*) / 47
Archaism (*Arhaism*) / 253
A Song (*Un cântec*) / 205
A Stanza of War (*Stanță de război*) / 264
A Stanza to Wine (*Stanță la vin*) / 225
Astonishing Snow . . . (*Ninge fenomenal . . .*) / 320
A Storm (*Furtună*) / 145
A Study (*Studiu*) / 222
At Edges (*În margini*) / 294
A Tale (*Poveste*) / 129
A Town Night (*Noapte de oraș*) / 248
At the Altar (*În altar*) / 160
At the End (*Din urmă*) / 166

At the Shore (*La țărm*) / 183
Autumn (*Toamnă*) (Pianos are weeping in town . . .) / 127
Autumn (*Toamnă*)
  (Resounding from the edge of town . . .) / 67
Autumn in the Town (*Toamnă în târg*) / 223
Autumn Lead (*Plumb de toamnă*) / 76
Autumn Lines (*Rânduri de toamnă*)
  (Alternative title [Yes] ([*Da*]) / 311
Autumn Nerves (*Nervi de toamnă*)
  (Autumn . . . I'm a child again . . .) / 327
Autumn Nerves (*Nervi de toamnă*)
  (In autumn, when the leaves . . .) / 85
Autumn Nerves (*Nervi de toamnă*)
  (It's autumn, it's rustle, it's sleep . . .) / 58
Autumn Nerves (*Nervi de toamnă*)
  (Leaden grass and strong air . . .) / 126
Autumn Notes (*Note de toamnă*)
  (Autumn in the garden . . .) / 87
Autumn Notes (*Note de toamnă*)
  (In the violet autumn . . .) / 119
Autumn Notes (*Note de toamnă*)
  (Silence . . . in the citadel . . .) / 60
Autumn Twilight (*Amurg de toamnă*) / 46
Autumn Waltz (*Vals de toamnă*) / 120

B
Ballet (*Balet*) / 103
Bisyllables and Monosyllables (*Bisilab și monosilab*) / 309
Black (*Negru*) / 53
Blood, Lead, Autumn (*Sânge, Plumb, Toamnă*) / 329
Bohemian (*Boemă*) / 238
Bountiful (*Belșug*) / 142

C
Chemistry (*Chimie*) / 283
Clouds Are Passing (*Trec nouri*) / 186
Cogito (*Cogito*) / 277

Cold (*Frig*) / 131
Contrast (*Contrast*) / 153
Controversy (*Controversă*) / 210
Count (*Compt*) / 271
Courage (*Curaj*) / 184
Crises (*Crize*) / 140

D
Darkness in the Town (*Negură-n oraș*) / 266
Days Pass (*Trec zile*) / 197
December (*Decembre*) / 52
Décor (*Decor*) / 41
Destiny (*Destin*) / 278
Dialogue (*Dialog*) / 313
Doina (*Doină*) (As much as I have tried ...) / 254
Doina (*Doină*) (Leaves crawling ...) / 245
Doina (*Doină*) (Poetry is silent ...) / 250
Dozing (*Dormitând*) / 107
Dust (*Pulvis*) / 65
Dying Autumn (*Toamnă murind*) / 325

E
Echo of a Love Song (*Ecou de romanță*) / 182
Echo of a Love Song (*Ecou de romanță*) / 190
Echo of Serenade (*Ecou de serenadă*) / 98
Ego (*Ego*) / 143
Egypt (*Egipet*) / 334
Elegy (*Elegie*) / 198
Emptiness (*Gol*) / 113
End of Autumn (*Sfârșit de toamnă*) / 200
Enough (*Destul*) / 164
Epitaph (*Epitaf*) / 163
Epode (*Epodă*) / 291
Evening (*Seară*) (Silence ...) / 280
Evening (*Seară*) (What sky is it ...) / 193
Excelsior (*Excelsior*) / 231
Exhausted (*Trudit*) / 69

F
Falling Heavily . . . (*Cade larg . . .*) / 306
Fanfare (*Fanfară*) / 112
Fantastic Verse (*Verset fantast*) / 300
Festive (*Festivă*) / 336
Fiefs (*Feude*) / 296
Finis (*Finis*) / 73
From Explorations (*Din explorări*)
　(That they too. . .) / 259
From Explorations (*Din explorări*)
　(. . . They also know . . .) / 267
From a Lyre (*Din liră*) / 173
From the Past (*Din vremuri*)
　(For a moment let me consider . . .) / 172
From the Past (*Din vremuri*) (It's cold, winter . . .) / 180
From the Informer (*Informativ*) / 265
From The Train (*Din tren*) / 260
Funeral March (*Marș funebru*) / 101

G
Gaudeamus (*Gaudeamus*) / 176
Gloss (*Glossă*) / 236
Grey (*Gri*) / 44

H
Hebrew Lady (*Ebreia*) / 330
High School (*Liceu*) / 138
Hygiene (*Igienă*) / 123
Hymn (*Imn*) / 147

I
I Am Silent (*Eu tac*) / 307
Ideal Verse (*Verset ideal*) / 297
Ideas (*Idei*) / 219
I Fell Asleep . . . (*Am adormit . . .*) / 308
In a Byre . . . (*Într-o șură . . .*) / 319
In Happiness (*În fericire*) / 209

Incident at the Ball (*Incident la bal*) / 279
In Somno (*In somno*) / 191
In the Garden (*În grădină*) / 48
In the Park (*În parc*) / 81
In the Village (*În sat*) / 257
In Winter (*În iarnă*) / 281
It's Raining (*Plouă*) / 78
It's Snowing (*Ninge*)
   (It's snowing. I stay at home, sick . . .) / 310
It's Snowing (*Ninge*)
   (When it starts to snow again . . .) / 122

J
July (*Cuptor*) / 66

L
Largo (*Largo*) / 77
Late Echo (*Ecou târziu*) / 185
Late Verse (*Verset târziu*) / 290
Lead (*Plumb*) / 39
Legend (*Legendă*) / 284
Let's Make Love (*Să ne iubim*) / 194
Libation (*Libelă*) / 286
Like a Wine (*Ca un vin*) / 321
Loneliness, I Didn't Want You
   (*Singurătate, nu te-am voit*) / 323
Lonely (*Singur*) / 68
Long Ago (*Demult*) / 203
Love Song (*Romanță*) (The scent of wet roses . . .) / 133
Love Song (*Romanță*)
   (When the moon is a rose of silver . . .) / 328

M
Medium Stanza (*Stanță medie*) / 251
Melancholy (*Melancolie*) / 56
Memento (*Memento*) / 195
Meridian (*Meridian*) / 227

Midnight (*Miezul nopții*) / 96
Modern (*Modernă*) / 235
Moment (*Moment*) / 288
Monosyllables of Autumn (*Monosilab de toamnă*) / 88
Morning (*Dimineață*) / 132
My Friend the Fig Tree (*Prietenul meu, smochinul*) / 339
Mystery (*Mister*) / 158
Mythology (*Mitologie*) / 276

N

Near Autumn (*Spre toamnă*) / 49
Neurosis (*Nevrosă*) / 54
New Year's Eve (*Revelion*) / 292
Newsreel (*Jurnal*) / 273
Nihil (*Nihil*) / 201
Nihil Novi (*Nihil novi*) / 228
Nocturnal Hibernation (*Hibernal noptat*) / 234
Nocturne (*Nocturnă*) (Forgetting it was coming . . .) / 89
Nocturne (*Nocturnă*) (I'm here . . .) / 75
Nocturne (*Nocturnă*) (In the citadel's night . . .) / 150
Nocturne (*Nocturnă*)
   (It is the music of autumn . . .) / 108
Nocturne (*Nocturnă*)
   (Night-light so full of scent . . .) / 114
Nocturne (*Nocturnă*)
   (No-one about . . . it's raining . . .) / 128
Nocturne (*Nocturnă*) (Oh, cease to sing
   you vagrant harmonies . . .) / 121
Noises (*Zgomote*) / 247

O

Obsessions (*Obsesii*) / 241
Oh, Twilights (*Oh, amurguri*) / 61
Old Stanza (*Stanță veche*) / 246
On the Hill (*Pe deal*) / 165
On the Horizon (*În zare*) / 289
One Midday of Summer (*Miazăzi de vară*) / 212

One Morning (*Matinală*) / 80
Otherwise (*Altfel*) / 71

P
Paling (*Pălind*) / 50
Pastel (*Pastel*) (— Adieu, the leaf falls . . .) / 105
Pastel (*Pastel*) (It is cold on the field . . .) / 285
Pastel (*Pastel*) (Poor poplars
  at the side of the mill . . .) / 187
Pastel (*Pastel*) (Silent places . . . the breeze . . .) / 208
Pastel (*Pastel*) (The horn of autumn . . .) / 40
Pastel (*Pastel*) (Too sullen . . .) / 263
Peace (*Pace*) / 275
Peepshow (*Panoramă*) / 72
Perhaps Tomorrow (*Ca mâine*) / 170
Perpetuum Mobile (*Perpetuum mobile*) / 233
Phantoms (*Strigoii*) / 100
Piano (*Piano*) / 157
Plain Style (*Stil simplu*) (In lyrical strains . . .) / 262
Plain Style (*Stil simplu*) (Like a soul . . .) / 255
Plain Style (*Stil simplu*) (Thunder . . .) / 258
Poem in the Mirror (*Poemă în oglindă*) / 82
Pro Arte (*Pro arte*) / 268
Prosaic Verse (*Verset prozaic*) / 298
Prose (*Proză*) (It rains . . .) / 141
Prose (*Proză*) (Love, like a Satyr . . .) / 139
Psalm (*Psalm*) / 152

R
Rarely (*Rar*) / 57
Real Stanza (*Stanță reală*) / 249
Reflections (*Reflecții*) / 242
Regret (*Regret*) / 169
Renunciation (*Renunțare*) / 188
Requiem (*Requiem*) / 213
Resignation (*Resemnare*) / 243
Restorations (*Restituiri*) / 295
Rotten Autumn (*Toamnă putredă*) / 305

S

Sad Evening (*Seară tristă*) / 59
Serenade (*Serenadă*) (A serenade of weeping ...) / 299
Serenade (*Serenadă*) (The moon poetizes ...) / 178
Sic Transit ... (*Sic transit* ...) / 217
Silence (*Tăcere*) / 179
Sine Die (*Sine die*) / 224
Slavic Verse (*Verset slav*) / 301
Sleet (*Moină*) / 55
Sometimes (*Vreodată*) / 196
Somewhere Else (*Aiurea*) / 151
Sonnet (*Sonet*) / 45
Spleen (*Spleen*) / 270
Springtime Nerves (*Nervi de primăvară*)
  (Melancholy has caught me ...) / 109
Springtime Nerves (*Nervi de primăvară*)
  (Spring's on the land ...) / 79
Springtime Notes (*Note de primăvară*) / 110
Stanza for Bacovia (*Stanță la Bacovia*) / 252
Stimulation (*Antrenare*) / 218
Stop Press (*De ultima oră*) / 232
Study (*Studiu*) / 274
Summer Night (*Noapte de vară*) / 207
Summer Twilight (*Amurg de vară*) / 111
Sunset (*Apus*) / 189

T

The Day of Wrath (*Dies Irae*) / 181
The Final Poem (*Poemă finală*) / 161
The First May Day (*Arminden*) / 221
The Shadow (*Umbra*) / 116
The Shoes (*Pantofii*) / 144
The Visit (*Visita*) / 229
The Worker's Serenade (*Serenada muncitorului*) / 104
Thoughts (*Gândiri*) / 282
To a Clown (*Unui clovn*) / 322
To a Maiden (*Unei fecioare*) / 118

To an Alcoholic (*Unui alcoolic*) / 332
Towards Spring (*Spre primăvară*) / 174
Twilight (*Amurg*) (At evening, on windows...) / 146
Twilight (*Amurg*)
  (Colourful bourgeois ladies passing...) / 156
Twilight (*Amurg*) (Like great tears of blood...) / 70
Twilight (*Amurg*) (New pale green crescent
  and lonely me...) / 95
Twilight (*Amurg*) (Sadness on the wind,
  sadness of the dead...) / 192
Twilight (*Amurg*) (Ravens fly — ah, 'The Ravens'...) / 42
Twilights (*Amurguri*) / 287

U
Urban Aesthetics (*Estetic urban*) / 226

V
Vae Soli (*Vae soli*) / 159
Vanitas (*Vanitas*) / 261
Veritas (*Veritas*) / 202
Verse Wandered Off (*Vers divagat*) / 331
Verses (*Versuri*) (Accords, arpeggios, harmonies...) / 199
Verses (*Versuri*) (From my life, I'd still like...) / 177
Violated Sepulcres (*Sepulcre violate*) / 162
Violet Twilight (*Amurg violet*) / 51
Vobiscum (*Vobiscum*) / 155

W
Warm Afternoon (*După-amiază caldă*) / 230
What Can I Do? (*Ce să fac?...*) / 318
When Alone (*Când singur*) / 171
White (*Alb*) / 84
Who Is Small... (*Cine-i mic...*) / 312
Who Sings... (*Cine cântă...*) / 317
Wind (*Vânt*) / 97
Winter Dialogue (*Dialog de iarnă*) / 148
Winter Twilight (*Amurg de iarnă*) / 62

Winter's Lead (*Plumb de iarnă*)
   (And again . . . the same hour . . .) / 125
Winter's Lead (*Plumb de iarnă*)
   (Age-old in silence . . .) / 86
Winter's Lead (*Plumb de iarnă*)
   (Lately, this winter . . .) / 74
With You (*Cu voi*) / 137
Worldly Stanza (*Stanță de lume*) / 269

Y

Yearning (*Alean*) / 63
Yellow Sparks (*Scântei galbene*)
   (A woman clad in mourning . . .) / 93
Yellow Sparks (*Scântei galbene*)
   (We'll say that autumn came . . .) / 106
You Died . . . (*Tu ai murit . . .*) / 326

Prose Poem Index

A Novel from the Past (*Nuvelă din trecut*) / 357
At the Coffee Party (*În cafeu*) / 345
In Vain (*În zadar*) / 347
Late (*Târziu*) / 343
Snow Storm (*Ninsoare*) / 353
The Black Cube (*Cubul negru*) / 348
The Thaw (*Moina*) / 355
Waves (*Valuri*) / 358
When Leaves Are Falling (*Când cad frunzele*) / 351

Short Prose Index

A Story I (*O poveste I*) / 363
A Story II (*O poveste II*) / 367
Bubi (*Bubi*) / 374
For Sale (*De Vânzare*) / 365

Little Old Grandmother Teaches Us a Game
  (*Ne-învață baba jocul*) / 372
Mother Hen with Chickens (*Cloșca cu pui*) / 378
The Bear (*Ursul*) / 370
The First Blade of Grass (*Primul fir de iarbă*) / 376
The Outlaw (*Proscrisul*) / 375
The People (*Poporul*) / 377
The Tramp (*Vagabondul*) / 373

Final Considerations (*Considerații finale*) / 381

Poetry Index in Romanian Listed Alphabetically

A
Aiurea / 151
Alb / 84
Alean / 63
Altfel / 71
Am adormit . . . / 308
Amurg (Crai nou, verde-pal, și eu singur . . .) / 95
Amurg (Cu lacrimi mari de sânge . . .) / 70
Amurg (Pe seară, la geamuri, un nour . . .) / 146
Amurg (Trec burgheze colorate . . .) / 156
Amurg (Trec corbii – ah, 'Corbii' . . .) / 42
Amurg (Tristeți pe vânt, tristeți de mort . . .) / 192
Amurg antic / 64
Amurg de iarnă / 62
Amurg de toamnă / 46
Amurg de vară / 111
Amurg violet / 51
Amurguri / 287
Antrenare / 218
Apus / 189
Arhaism / 253
Arminden / 221

B
Baladă (Clopot de alarmă la mânăstire . . .) / 211
Baladă (O noapte de sineală din vremi . . .) / 154
Balet / 103
Belșug / 142
Bisilab și monosilab / 309
Boemă / 238

C
Ca mâine / 170
Ca un vin / 321

Cade larg... / 306
Când singur / 171
Ce să fac?... / 318
Chimie / 283
Cine cântă... / 317
Cine-i mic... / 312
Cogito / 277
Compt / 271
Contrast / 153
Controversă / 210
Crize / 140
Cu voi / 137
Cuptor / 66
Curaj / 184

D
De artă / 237
De iarnă (Chiciură...) / 272
De iarnă (Cum ninge repede, apoi încet...) / 115
De iarnă (În ecouri bocitoare...) / 117
De iarnă (Un hoit, un corb, un câmp și eu...) / 175
De ultima oră / 232
Decembre / 52
Decor / 41
Demult / 203
Destin / 278
Destul / 164
Deși nimic / 244
Dialog / 313
Dialog de iarnă / 148
Dies Irae / 181
Dimineață / 132
Din explorări (Că, și ei...) / 259
Din explorări (... Știu și ei...) / 267
Din liră / 173
Din tren / 260
Din urmă / 166

Din vremuri (E frig, iarnă...) / 180
Din vremuri (Un moment, să gândesc...) / 172
Doină (Dintre câte-am încercat...) / 254
Doină (Frunze se târăsc...) / 245
Doină (Poezia tace...) / 250
Dormitând / 107
După-amiază caldă / 230

E
Ebreia / 330
Ecou de romanță / 182
Ecou de romanță / 190
Ecou de serenadă / 98
Ecou târziu / 185
Egipet / 334
Ego / 143
Elegie / 198
Epitaf / 163
Epodă / 291
Estetic urban / 226
Eu tac / 307
Excelsior / 231

F
Fanfară / 112
Festivă / 336
Feude / 296
Finis / 73
Frig / 131
Furtună / 145

G
Gaudeamus / 176
Gândiri / 282
Glossă / 236
Gol / 113
Gri / 44

H
Hibernal noptat / 234

I
Idei / 219
Igienă / 123
Imn / 147
In somno / 191
Incident la bal / 279
Informativ / 265

Î
În altar / 160
În fericire / 209
În grădină / 48
În iarnă / 281
În margini) / 294
În parc / 81
În sat / 257
În zare / 289
Între ziduri / 130
Într-o șură . . . / 319

J
Jurnal / 273

L
La țărm / 183
Lacustră / 43
Largo / 77
Legendă / 204
Legendă / 284
Libelă / 286
Liceu / 138

M
Marș funebru / 101
Matinală / 80

Melancolie / 56
Memento / 195
Meridian / 227
Miazăzi de vară / 212
Miezul nopții / 96
Mister / 158
Mitologie / 276
Modernă / 235
Moină / 55
Moment / 288
Monosilab de toamnă / 88

N
Negru / 53
Negură-n oraș / 266
Nervi de primăvară (Melancolia m-a prins pe stradă...) / 109
Nervi de primăvară (Primăvară...) / 79
Nervi de toamnă (E toamnă, e foșnet, e somn...) / 58
Nervi de toamnă (Iarbă de plumb și aer tare) / 126
Nervi de toamnă (La toamnă, când frunză va...) / 85
Nervi de toamnă (Toamnă, iar sunt copil...) / 327
Nevrosă / 54
Nihil / 201
Nihil novi / 228
Ninge (Când iar începe-a ninge...) / 122
Ninge (Ninge. Bolnav stau în casă...) / 310
Ninge fenomenal... / 320
Noapte / 99
Noapte de oraș / 248
Noapte de vară / 207
Nocturnă (Clar de noapte parfumat...) / 114
Nocturnă (E-o muzică de toamnă...) / 108
Nocturnă (Fug rătăcind în noaptea...) / 150
Nocturnă (Nu e nimeni... plouă...) / 128
Nocturnă (O, nu mai cânta, harmonie...) / 121
Nocturnă (Stau...și moina cade, apă, glod...) / 75

Nocturnă (Uitarea venea... a venit...) / 89
Note de primăvară / 110
Note de toamnă (Toamna-n grădină și-acordă vioara...) / 87
Note de toamnă (În toamna violetă, compozitori...) / 119
Note de toamnă (Tăcere... e toamnă în cetate...) / 60

O
Obsesii / 241
Oh, amurguri / 61

P
Pace / 275
Panoramă / 72
Pantofii / 144
Pastel (— Adio, pică frunza...) / 105
Pastel (Buciumă toamna...) / 40
Pastel (E frig, la câmp...) / 285
Pastel (Prea ursuz...) / 263
Pastel (Sărmanii plopi de lângă moară...) / 187
Pastel (Tăcute locuri... curent...) / 208
Pălind / 50
Pe deal / 165
Perpetuum mobile / 233
Piano / 157
Plouă / 78
Plumb / 39
Plumb de iarnă (Iarna, de-o vreme...) / 74
Plumb de iarnă (Ninge secular, tăcere...) / 86
Plumb de iarnă (Și iar... aceeași oră...) / 125
Plumb de toamnă / 76
Poemă finală / 161
Poemă în oglindă / 82
Poveste / 129
Prietenul meu, smochinul / 339
Pro arte / 268
Proză (Amorul, hodos ca un satir...) / 139
Proză (Plouă...) / 141

Psalm / 152
Pulvis / 65

R
Rar / 57
Rânduri de toamnă / 311
Reflecții / 242
Regret / 169
Renunțare / 188
Requiem / 213
Resemnare / 243
Restituiri / 295
Revelion / 292
Romanță (Când luna e o rază de argint...) / 328
Romanță (Parfumul rozelor ude...) / 133

S
Să ne iubim / 194
Sânge, Plumb, Toamnă / 329
Scântei galbene (O femeie în doliu pe stradă...) / 93
Scântei galbene (Vom spune că toamna a venit...) / 106
Seară (Ce este cerul — ori ziua a trecut...) / 193
Seară (Liniște...) / 280
Seară tristă / 59
Sepulcre violate / 162
Serenada muncitorului / 104
Serenadă / 299
Sfârșit de toamnă / 200
Sic transit... / 217
Sine die / 224
Singur (Potop, cad stele albe de cristal...) / 68
Singur (Odaia mea mă înspăimântă...) / 94
Singurătate, nu te-am voit / 323
Sonet / 45
Spleen / 270
Spre primăvară / 174
Spre toamnă / 49

Stanță de lume / 269
Stanță de război / 264
Stanță la Bacovia / 252
Stanță la vin / 225
Stanță medie / 251
Stanță reală / 249
Stanță veche / 246
Stil simplu (Ce suflet...) / 255
Stil simplu (Duruieli...) / 258
Stil simplu (În sunete lirice...) / 262
Strigoii / 100
Studiu (Când căutam...) / 274
Studiu (Lângă strune de vioară...) / 222

Ș
Și ce... / 333
Și dacă / 338
Și ninge... / 124
Și toate / 206

T
Tablou de iarnă / 47
Tăcere / 179
Toamnă (Clavirele plâng în oraș...) / 127
Toamnă (Răsună din margine de târg...) / 67
Toamnă în târg / 223
Toamnă murind / 325
Toamnă putredă / 305
Trec nouri / 186
Trec zile / 197
Trudit / 69
Tu ai murit... / 326

U
Umbra / 116
Un cântec / 205
Unei fecioare / 118

Unui alcoolic / 332
Unui clovn / 322

V
Vae soli / 159
Vals de toamnă / 120
Vanitas / 261
Vânt / 97
Veritas / 202
Vers divagat / 331
Verset fantast / 300
Verset ideal / 297
Verset prozaic / 298
Verset slav / 301
Verset târziu / 290
Versuri (Acorduri, arpegii, armonii . . .) / 199
Versuri (Un cântec trist din liră . . .) / 177
Visita / 229
Vobiscum / 155
Vreodată / 196

Z
Zgomote / 247

Prose Poem Titles in Romanian

Când cad frunzele / 351
Cubul negru / 348
În cafeu / 345
În zadar / 347
Moina / 355
Ninsoare / 353
Nuvelă din trecut / 357
Târziu / 343
Valuri / 358

Short Story Titles in Romanian

Bubi / 374
Cloșca cu pui / 378
De vânzare / 365
Ne-învață baba jocul / 372
O poveste I / 363
O Poveste II / 367
Poporul / 377
Primul fir de iarbă / 376
Proscrisul / 375
Ursul / 370
Vagabondul / 373

       Considerații finale / 381